CW00742595

Revise
Maths

KS2: YEAR 6

Age 10–11

Paul Broadbent and Peter Patilla

First published 2007
exclusively for WHSmith by
Hodder Murray, a member of the Hodder Headline group
338 Euston Road
London
NW1 3BH

Impression number   10 9 8 7 6 5 4 3 2 1
Year   2008 2007
Text and illustrations © Hodder Education 2007

All rights reserved. No part of this publication may be reproduced or transmitted in any form or by any means, electronic or mechanical, including photocopying, recording or any information storage and retrieval system, without permission in writing from the publisher or under licence from the Copyright Licensing Agency Limited. Further details of such licences (for reprographic reproduction) may be obtained from the Copyright Licensing Agency Limited, Saffron House, 6–10 Kirby Street, London EC1N 8TS.

A CIP record for this book is available from the British Library.

Cover illustration by Sally Newton Illustrations

Typeset by Fakenham Photosetting Limited, Fakenham, Norfolk

ISBN – 13   978 0 34094278 9

Printed and bound in Italy.

Contents

The *WHS Revise* series

The *WHS Revise* books enable you to help your child revise and practise important skills taught in school. These skills form part of the National Curriculum and will help your child to improve his or her Maths and English.

Testing in schools

During their time at school all children will undergo a variety of tests. Regular testing is a feature of all schools. It is carried out:

- *informally* – in everyday classroom activities your child's teacher is continually assessing and observing your child's performance in a general way
- *formally* – more regular formal testing helps the teacher check your child's progress in specific areas.

Testing is important because:

- it provides evidence of your child's achievement and progress
- it helps the teacher decide which skills to focus on with your child
- it helps compare how different children are progressing.

The importance of revision

Regular revision is important to ensure your child remembers and practises skills he or she has been taught. These books will help your child revise and test his or her knowledge of some of the things he or she will be expected to know. They will help you prepare your child to be in a better position to face tests in school with confidence.

How to use this book

Units

This book is divided into forty units, each focusing on one key skill. Each unit begins with a **Remember** section, which introduces and revises essential information about the particular skill covered. If possible, read and discuss this with your child to ensure he or she understands it.

This is followed by a **Have a go** section, which contains a number of activities to help your child revise the topic thoroughly and use the skill effectively. Usually, your child should be able to do these activities fairly independently.

Revision tests

There are four revision tests in the book (pages 46–53). These test the skills covered in the preceding units and assess your child's progress and understanding. They can be marked by you or by your child. Your child should fill in his or her test score for each test in the space provided. This will provide a visual record of your child's progress and an instant sense of confidence and achievement.

Parents' notes

The parents' notes (on pages 54–57) provide you with brief information on each skill and explain why it is important.

Answers

Answers to the unit questions and tests may be found on pages 58–64.

Unit 1: Decimal numbers

Remember

The **decimal point** separates **whole numbers** from **tenths**.

tens	ones	tenths	hundredths	thousandths
1	4 •	3	5	2
10 $+$ 4		$\frac{3}{10}$ $+$	$\frac{5}{100}$ $+$	$\frac{2}{1000}$

Have a go

1 Write the value of the red digit as a fraction.

a 3.68 _____

b 14.05 _____

c 28.314 _____

d 20.062 _____

e 9.325 _____

f 53.709 _____

g 0.054 _____

h 31.624 _____

2 Write a matching decimal for each arrow.

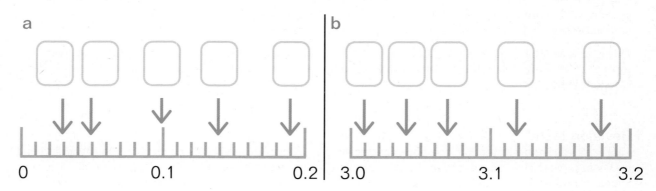

3 Rearrange this set to make a decimal number as near as possible to 1. There must be one digit in front of the decimal point.

6, 0, 8, 1

Remember

Multiplying and dividing decimals by 10 and 100 uses the same rules as whole numbers.

To multiply by 10:
Move the digits one place to the left and fill the space with a zero.

$\times$ 10   3 . 6 4
                  3 6 . 4 0

To divide by 10:
Move the digits one place to the right.

$\div$ 10   1 2 . 8
                  1 . 2 8

To multiply by 100:
Move the digits two places to the left and fill the spaces with zeros.

$\times$ 100   0 . 2 9
                    2 9 . 0 0

To divide by 100:
Move the digits two places to the right.

$\div$ 100   1 5 . 6
                   0 . 1 5 6

Putting a zero on the end of a decimal doesn't change the number.
So, 1.5 is the same as 1.50 and 1.500.

Have a go

1 Write the answers.

a Multiply each of these by 10:	b Multiply each of these by 100:	c Divide each of these by 10:	d Divide each of these by 100:
4.2 ➡ _____	4.35 ➡ _____	18.4 ➡ _____	19.1 ➡ _____
19.5 ➡ _____	9.6 ➡ _____	13.8 ➡ _____	80 ➡ _____
0.75 ➡ _____	2.51 ➡ _____	9.6 ➡ _____	71.5 ➡ _____
1.873 ➡ _____	0.072 ➡ _____	0.25 ➡ _____	8.2 ➡ _____
0.366 ➡ _____	3.406 ➡ _____	7.03 ➡ _____	0.7 ➡ _____

2 Write the missing numbers in these chains.

a 4.5 $\div$ 10 ➡ _____ $\div$ 10 ➡ _____ $\times$ 100 ➡ _____

b 2.06 $\times$ 10 ➡ _____ $\div$ 100 ➡ _____ $\times$ 10 ➡ _____

c 0.33 $\div$ 10 ➡ _____ $\times$ 100 ➡ _____ $\div$ 10 ➡ _____

d 1.62 $\times$ 100 ➡ _____ $\div$ 10 ➡ _____ $\div$ 100 ➡ _____

Unit 3: Ordering numbers

Remember

Putting **decimals** in order is just like putting whole numbers in order – you need to look carefully at the value of each digit.

To help you to put them in order of size, first write them out one under the other, **lining up the decimal points**.

Example 3.95, 2.61, 3.2, 2.06, 2.6

3.95		2.06
2.61		2.6
3.2	⟶	2.61
2.06		3.2
2.6		3.95

Then compare each digit value and rearrange the numbers until they are in order.

Have a go

① Write these numbers in order, starting with the smallest.

a | 5.35 | 2.05 | 5.03 | 5.23 | 5.7 |
| | | | | |

b | 2.81 | 2.68 | 3.88 | 1.27 | 1.3 |
| | | | | |

c | 40.77 | 47.07 | 47.7 | 4.77 | 47.4 |
| | | | | |

d | 23.11 | 2.06 | 2.83 | 2.3 | 23.3 |
| | | | | |

e | 6.12 | 6.5 | 6.65 | 7.03 | 6.21 |
| | | | | |

f | 19.5 | 20.05 | 20.9 | 19.29 | 20.53 |
| | | | | |

g | 3.81 | 3.68 | 3.9 | 3.23 | 3.09 |
| | | | | |

h | 14.37 | 13.09 | 14.4 | 14.09 | 13.95 |
| | | | | |

② Use the digits 3, 6, 9, 2 and a decimal point. Make eight numbers between 1 and 10. Write them in order, starting with the smallest.

Unit 4: Number sequences

Remember

To work out the **pattern** in a **sequence**, look at the **difference** between each number.

The pattern or rule is +3

The pattern or rule is −8

Remember to include zero when you're looking at negative numbers in a sequence.

Have a go

Write the missing numbers and the rule. The first one has been done for you.

a   −16   −11   −6   −1   4   9   Rule: __+5__

b   −15   ☐   ☐   18   29   ☐   Rule: _____

c   ☐   −2   ☐   −10   −14   ☐   Rule: _____

d   ☐   ☐   5   25   ☐   65   Rule: _____

e   ☐   0   −7   ☐   ☐   −28   Rule: _____

f   40   28   ☐   4   ☐   ☐   Rule: _____

g   ☐   ☐   8   38   ☐   98   Rule: _____

h   16   ☐   ☐   −11   −20   ☐   Rule: _____

Remember

You can use function machines to create patterns of numbers like those below.

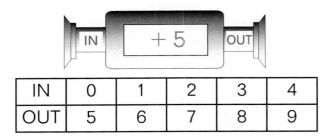

IN	0	1	2	3	4
OUT	5	6	7	8	9

IN	0	1	2	3	4
OUT	1	3	5	7	9

Have a go

1 Complete each table of results.

a
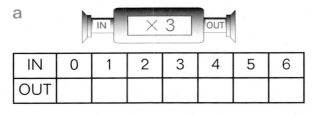

IN	0	1	2	3	4	5	6
OUT							

b
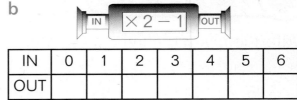

IN	0	1	2	3	4	5	6
OUT							

c
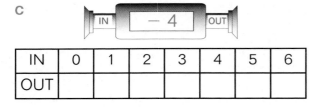

IN	0	1	2	3	4	5	6
OUT							

d
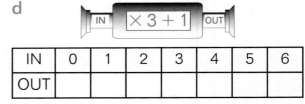

IN	0	1	2	3	4	5	6
OUT							

e
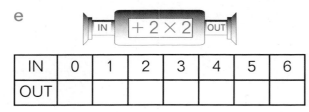

IN	0	1	2	3	4	5	6
OUT							

f
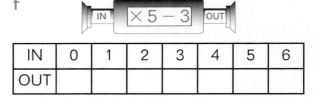

IN	0	1	2	3	4	5	6
OUT							

2 Write the functions for each of these tables of results.

a
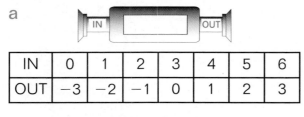

IN	0	1	2	3	4	5	6
OUT	−3	−2	−1	0	1	2	3

b
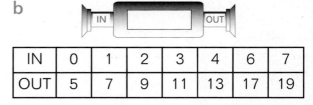

IN	0	1	2	3	4	6	7
OUT	5	7	9	11	13	17	19

c
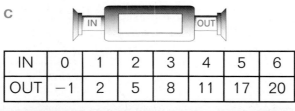

IN	0	1	2	3	4	5	6
OUT	−1	2	5	8	11	17	20

d
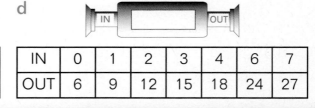

IN	0	1	2	3	4	6	7
OUT	6	9	12	15	18	24	27

Unit 6: Multiples

Remember

A **multiple** of a number is found by multiplying that number by any other. So the multiples of 3 are 3, 6, 9, 12, 15, . . . and they go on and on.

There are rules to test whether a number is a multiple of 2, 3, 4, 5, 6, 8, 9, or 10. For example, a whole number is a multiple of:

3 – if the sum of its digits can be divided by 3
e.g. 615 (6 + 1 + 5 = 12), 4401 (4 + 4 + 0 + 1 = 9)

4 – if the last two digits can be divided by 4
e.g. 524, 680, 3312

6 – if it is even and divisible by 3
e.g. 738, 702, 516

Do you know the rules for multiples of 2, 5 and 10?

Have a go

1. Circle the odd one out in each set.

a Multiples of 3

126   136   4023
384   7116

b Multiples of 4
7424   6004   8060
944   4314

c Multiples of 6
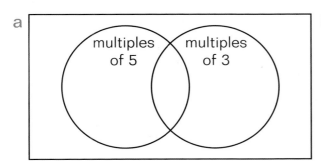
270   3012   7290
3462   4124

d Multiples of 9
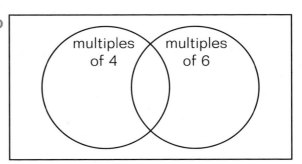
423   4104   7920
207   3509

2. Write the numbers 100 to 120 in each of these Venn diagrams.

a
multiples of 5   multiples of 3

b
multiples of 4   multiples of 6

3. 360 is a multiple of many numbers. Tick the numbers below that 360 can be exactly divided by:

2 ◯   3 ◯   4 ◯   5 ◯   6 ◯   7 ◯   8 ◯   9 ◯   10 ◯

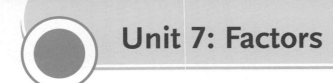

Unit 7: Factors

Remember

Factors are numbers that divide exactly into other numbers. It is useful to put them in pairs. Factors of 12 in pairs are (1 and 12) (2 and 6) (3 and 4). So 12 has 6 factors.

A number that has only two factors – 1 and itself – is called a **prime number**. The only factors of 13 are (1 and 13), so 13 is a prime number.

① Write all the pairs of factors of each of these.

a 15
(___,___)
(___,___)

b 8
(___,___)
(___,___)

c 28
(___,___)
(___,___)
(___,___)

d 45
(___,___)
(___,___)
(___,___)

e 20
(___,___)
(___,___)
(___,___)

f 32
(___,___)
(___,___)
(___,___)

g 30
(___,___)
(___,___)
(___,___)
(___,___)

h 42
(___,___)
(___,___)
(___,___)
(___,___)

i 40
(___,___)
(___,___)
(___,___)
(___,___)

j 48
(___,___)
(___,___)
(___,___)
(___,___)
(___,___)

② Write the factors for these square numbers in order.

a 25 [   ]

b 36 [   ]

c 49 [   ]

d 64 [   ]

What is special about the number of factors for square numbers? _____

③ Answer these questions about this set of numbers.

16	17	18	19	20	21

a Which two numbers are prime numbers? _____ and _____

b Which number is a factor of 100? _____

c Which number is a square number? _____

d Which two numbers are a multiple of 3? _____ and _____

e Which number is a multiple of both 6 and 9? _____

f Which number has four factors? _____

Unit 8: Fractions

Remember

Fractions have a **numerator** and a **denominator**.

numerator ⟶ $\frac{3}{4}$ ⟵ denominator

Equivalent fractions are worth the same.
You usually write fractions using the smallest possible denominator.

These are part of the $\frac{1}{2}$ family.

Have a go

1 Complete these equivalent fractions.

a $\frac{4}{\Box} = \frac{2}{3}$

b $\frac{2}{10} = \frac{1}{\Box}$

c $\frac{\Box}{12} = \frac{1}{4}$

d $\frac{6}{\Box} = \frac{1}{2}$

e $\frac{\Box}{15} = \frac{1}{3}$

f $\frac{2}{8} = \frac{\Box}{4}$

g $\frac{15}{20} = \frac{3}{\Box}$

h $\frac{9}{\Box} = \frac{1}{2}$

2 Write three members of each of these fraction families.

a $\frac{1}{3}$ ▨▦ ⬜ ⬜ ⬜

b $\frac{1}{4}$ ▨▦ ⬜ ⬜ ⬜

c $\frac{3}{4}$ ▨▦ ⬜ ⬜ ⬜

d $\frac{2}{3}$ ▨▦ ⬜ ⬜ ⬜

3 Circle the odd one out in each set.

a
$\frac{12}{20}$ $\frac{3}{5}$
$\frac{9}{15}$ $\frac{15}{20}$ $\frac{6}{10}$

b
$\frac{12}{20}$ $\frac{3}{4}$
$\frac{6}{8}$
$\frac{18}{24}$ $\frac{9}{12}$

c
$\frac{2}{6}$ $\frac{7}{21}$
$\frac{1}{3}$
$\frac{9}{24}$ $\frac{6}{18}$

Unit 9: Ordering fractions

Remember

Putting fractions in order of size is easy if they all have the same **denominator**. You just need to put the **numerators** in order.

These are in order, starting with the smallest: $\frac{1}{8}, \frac{3}{8}, \frac{5}{8}, \frac{7}{8}$.

If a set of fractions have different denominators, then you need to change them so that they are all the same by making **equivalent fractions**. To do this, look at the denominators and find a number that they can all divide into.

Example
Put these in order, starting with the smallest: $\frac{2}{5}, \frac{7}{10}, \frac{1}{2}, \frac{3}{5}$.

The denominators all divide into 10, so change them all to tenths and then write them in order:

$$\frac{2}{5} = \frac{4}{10} \qquad \frac{1}{2} = \frac{5}{10} \qquad \frac{3}{5} = \frac{6}{10} \qquad \frac{7}{10} = \frac{7}{10}$$

Have a go

① Circle the larger fraction in each pair.

a $\frac{1}{2}$ or $\frac{5}{8}$ b $\frac{1}{5}$ or $\frac{3}{10}$ c $\frac{5}{6}$ or $\frac{7}{12}$ d $\frac{3}{4}$ or $\frac{7}{8}$ e $\frac{1}{3}$ or $\frac{5}{6}$

f $\frac{1}{2}$ or $\frac{1}{3}$ g $\frac{1}{4}$ or $\frac{1}{5}$ h $\frac{2}{3}$ or $\frac{3}{5}$ i $\frac{2}{3}$ or $\frac{3}{4}$ j $\frac{5}{6}$ or $\frac{3}{4}$

② Write each set of fractions in order, starting with the smallest.

a $\frac{1}{3}, \frac{3}{4}, \frac{5}{12}, \frac{1}{2}, \frac{5}{6}$

b $\frac{1}{15}, \frac{2}{3}, \frac{4}{5}, \frac{1}{3}, \frac{7}{15}$

c $\frac{3}{4}, \frac{1}{6}, \frac{7}{12}, \frac{2}{3}, \frac{1}{2}$

d $\frac{2}{3}, \frac{5}{9}, \frac{1}{6}, \frac{2}{9}, \frac{1}{2}$

e $\frac{7}{10}, \frac{3}{5}, \frac{1}{2}, \frac{3}{4}, \frac{4}{5}$

f $\frac{2}{3}, \frac{3}{8}, \frac{5}{6}, \frac{3}{4}, \frac{5}{8}$

Unit 10: Fractions and decimals

Remember

Try to remember these **fractions** and **decimals**.

$\frac{1}{2} = 0.5$ $\frac{1}{4} = 0.25$ $\frac{1}{5} = 0.2$ $\frac{1}{10} = 0.1$ $\frac{3}{4} = 0.75$

$\frac{1}{3} = 0.333\ldots$ $\frac{2}{3} = 0.666\ldots$

These two are **recurring** – they go on and on.

You can change decimals into fractions by dividing by 10 or 100. For example:

$0.4 = \frac{4}{10} = \frac{2}{5}$
$0.75 = \frac{75}{100} = \frac{3}{4}$

You can change fractions into decimals by dividing. For example:

$\frac{3}{5} = 5\overline{)3.0}^{\,0.6}$ $\frac{7}{8} = 8\overline{)7.000}^{\,0.875}$

Have a go

1 Change these to decimals.

a $\frac{2}{5} =$ b $\frac{7}{10} =$ c $\frac{1}{8} =$ d $\frac{4}{5} =$ e $\frac{5}{8} =$

2 Change these to fractions.

a $0.9 =$ b $0.3 =$ c $0.85 =$ d $0.15 =$ e $0.01 =$

3 Join the fractions to the equivalent decimals.

3.2 $3\frac{1}{4}$ 3.5   2.7 $2\frac{3}{4}$

$2\frac{4}{5}$ 2.8 $3\frac{1}{5}$ $3\frac{2}{5}$ 3.4

2.75 $3\frac{1}{2}$ 3.25 $2\frac{7}{10}$ 2.125 $2\frac{1}{8}$

Unit 11: Percentages

Remember

Percent means 'out of 100' – **percentages** are **fractions out of 100**.
The sign for percent is %.

$$25\% = \frac{25}{100} = \frac{1}{4}$$

Numbers to be changed to percentages must be out of 100.
Example:
In a spelling test you score 8 out of 10.

$$\frac{8}{10} = \frac{80}{100} = 80\%$$

Have a go

1 Change these test scores to percentages.

a 7 out of 10 = _____ %   b 15 out of 20 = _____ %

c 20 out of 25 = _____ %   d 34 out of 50 = _____ %

e 19 out of 20 = _____ %   f 15 out of 25 = _____ %

g 3 out of 20 = _____ %   h 23 out of 25 = _____ %

2 Complete each fraction.

a $75\% = \dfrac{\bigcirc}{4}$ b $20\% = \dfrac{\bigcirc}{5}$ c $15\% = \dfrac{\bigcirc}{20}$ d $90\% = \dfrac{\bigcirc}{10}$

e $45\% = \dfrac{\bigcirc}{20}$ f $25\% = \dfrac{\bigcirc}{4}$ g $60\% = \dfrac{\bigcirc}{5}$ h $98\% = \dfrac{\bigcirc}{50}$

3 Write the percentages given in these headlines.

a There was a one-in-a-hundred chance of finding the diamond
_____ %

b Eight out of ten owners said their cats prefer fresh food to tinned food
_____ %

c Four in five people read our newspaper! The rest look at the pictures . . .
_____ %

d Fifty people were questioned and thirty-five of them provided useful information
_____ %

e Only eighteen of the twenty-five diners were satisfied with the food
_____ %

f Liverpool have won sixteen of their last twenty matches and are now favourites for the title
_____ %

Unit 12: Percentages of amounts

Remember

Try these different methods of working out percentages of amounts.

Example What is 20% of £70?
With questions like this, the word 'of' means **multiply**.

Method 1
Change to a fraction and
work it out:

$\frac{20}{100} \times £70 = \frac{2}{10}$ of £70 = £14

Method 2
Use 10% to work it out, dividing by 10:
10% of £70 is £7

So, 20% of £70 is double that: £14
To find 5%, remember that it is half of 10%.

Have a go

1 Calculate the percentages of these amounts.

a £1.40	b £3.80	c £5.20	d £12.60
10% ➡ _____	10% ➡ _____	10% ➡ _____	10% ➡ _____
20% ➡ _____	20% ➡ _____	20% ➡ _____	20% ➡ _____
5% ➡ _____	5% ➡ _____	5% ➡ _____	5% ➡ _____

e £28	f £23.60	g £19	h £21.20
10% ➡ _____	10% ➡ _____	10% ➡ _____	10% ➡ _____
20% ➡ _____	20% ➡ _____	20% ➡ _____	20% ➡ _____
5% ➡ _____	5% ➡ _____	5% ➡ _____	5% ➡ _____

2 Answer these questions.

a A piece of tape is 200 cm long. If 30% is cut off, what length of tape has been cut? _____

b A water tank holds 300 litres. If it is 25% full, how much water is in the tank? _____

c There were 50 chairs in a hall. If 70% of them were stacked, how many were left over? _____

d There are 40 children at a party. If 60% of them are girls, how many boys are there? _____

Unit 13: Number facts

Remember

You need to know all your **number bonds** to 20 for **addition** and **subtraction**.
Use this number grid to help you learn the facts.
Use them to learn other trickier facts.

+	0	1	2	3	4	5	6	7	8	9	10
0	0	1	2	3	4	5	6	7	8	9	10
1	1	2	3	4	5	6	7	8	9	10	11
2	2	3	4	5	6	7	8	9	10	11	12
3	3	4	5	6	7	8	9	10	11	12	13
4	4	5	6	7	8	9	10	11	12	13	14
5	5	6	7	8	9	10	11	12	13	14	15
6	6	7	8	9	10	11	12	13	14	15	16
7	7	8	9	10	11	12	13	14	15	16	17
8	8	9	10	11	12	13	14	15	16	17	18
9	9	10	11	12	13	14	15	16	17	18	19
10	10	11	12	13	14	15	16	17	18	19	20

$7 + 8 = 15$
$17 + 8 = 25$
$70 + 80 = 150$

$15 - 7 = 8$
$25 - 7 = 18$
$150 - 70 = 80$

Have a go

1 Write the missing numbers.

a
$6 + \boxed{} = 14$

$6 + \boxed{} = 24$

$60 + \boxed{} = 140$

b
$9 + \boxed{} = 16$

$9 + \boxed{} = 36$

$90 + \boxed{} = 160$

c
$\boxed{} + 8 = 15$

$\boxed{} + 8 = 45$

$\boxed{} + 80 = 150$

d
$\boxed{} + 4 = 12$

$\boxed{} + 4 = 32$

$\boxed{} + 40 = 120$

e
$18 - \boxed{} = 9$

$48 - \boxed{} = 39$

$180 - \boxed{} = 90$

f
$15 - \boxed{} = 6$

$35 - \boxed{} = 26$

$150 - \boxed{} = 60$

g
$\boxed{} - 4 = 7$

$\boxed{} - 4 = 17$

$\boxed{} - 40 = 70$

h
$\boxed{} - 5 = 7$

$\boxed{} - 5 = 37$

$\boxed{} - 50 = 70$

2 Use a timer. Answer these as quickly as you can.

a $8 + 7 = \underline{}$ b $9 - 3 = \underline{}$ c $9 + 8 = \underline{}$ d $6 + 6 = \underline{}$ e $17 - 9 = \underline{}$

$5 + 8 = \underline{}$ $16 - 7 = \underline{}$ $4 + 8 = \underline{}$ $14 - 8 = \underline{}$ $11 - 5 = \underline{}$

$13 - 9 = \underline{}$ $5 + 6 = \underline{}$ $9 + 7 = \underline{}$ $9 - 4 = \underline{}$ $8 + 8 = \underline{}$

$14 - 7 = \underline{}$ $7 + 6 = \underline{}$ $9 + 9 = \underline{}$ $9 + 5 = \underline{}$ $13 - 6 = \underline{}$

Try it again. Can you beat your best time?

Unit 14: Brackets

Remember

When part of a calculation is in brackets, you **work out the brackets part first**.

$15 - (6 + 8) = 15 - 14 = 1$

$(18 - 9) + (5 \times 3) = 9 + 15 = 24$

Have a go

1 Answer these. Remember to work out the brackets first.

a $19 + (6 \times 5) =$ ☐

b $15 - (6 + 5) =$ ☐

c $8 \times (12 - 9) =$ ☐

d $15 + (11 - 5) =$ ☐

e $21 - (6 \times 3) =$ ☐

f $(4 \times 6) + (16 - 5) =$ ☐

g $(7 + 5) - (16 - 9) =$ ☐

h $(8 + 7) - (24 \div 3) =$ ☐

i $(6 \times 3) - (15 - 9) =$ ☐

2 Put brackets into each of these to make the largest answers possible.

a $7 + 3 \times 8 =$ ☐

b $6 - 2 \times 8 + 3 =$ ☐

c $8 + 4 - 2 \times 3 =$ ☐

d $8 + 10 \div 2 \times 3 =$ ☐

e $40 \div 5 \times 4 =$ ☐

3 Choose from $+, -, \times, \div$.
Complete these number sentences.

a 5 ☐ $(3$ ☐ $9) = 60$

b 3 ☐ $(19$ ☐ $8) = 14$

c $(6$ ☐ $4)$ ☐ $(16$ ☐ $4) = 20$

d $(4$ ☐ $5)$ ☐ $(3$ ☐ $8) = 44$

e $(9$ ☐ $8)$ ☐ $(2$ ☐ $6) = 5$

f 8 ☐ $(7$ ☐ $3)$ ☐ $9 = 20$

Unit 15: Addition

$$\begin{array}{r} 4209 \\ 2833 \\ + 1694 \\ \hline 8736 \\ \hline {\scriptstyle 1\ 1\ 1} \end{array}$$

● Remember

When you **add** numbers that are too large to total in your head, use a **written method**, like this.

For this method it is easier to start with the units $9 + 3 + 4 = 16$. Write the 6 and remember to add the 10 in the next column. This continues for each column to the thousands.

● Have a go

1 Answer each of these.

a
$$\begin{array}{r} 4198 \\ + 3206 \\ \hline \end{array}$$

b
$$\begin{array}{r} 4734 \\ + 2966 \\ \hline \end{array}$$

c
$$\begin{array}{r} 1877 \\ + 2091 \\ \hline \end{array}$$

d
$$\begin{array}{r} 3072 \\ + 5637 \\ \hline \end{array}$$

e
$$\begin{array}{r} 1897 \\ + 6794 \\ \hline \end{array}$$

f
$$\begin{array}{r} 2785 \\ + 1934 \\ + 3497 \\ \hline \end{array}$$

g
$$\begin{array}{r} 4105 \\ + 6783 \\ + 1346 \\ \hline \end{array}$$

h
$$\begin{array}{r} 2155 \\ + 3905 \\ + 2086 \\ \hline \end{array}$$

i
$$\begin{array}{r} 1037 \\ + 8489 \\ + 3856 \\ \hline \end{array}$$

j
$$\begin{array}{r} 3267 \\ + 5409 \\ + 4564 \\ \hline \end{array}$$

2 Write the missing numbers.

a
$$\begin{array}{r} 4\ \square\ 7\ 2 \\ + 1\ 6\ 8\ \square \\ \hline 6\ 0\ \square\ 7 \end{array}$$

b
$$\begin{array}{r} \square\ 8\ 0\ 5 \\ + 3\ 9\ \square\ 7 \\ \hline 8\ 8\ 0\ \square \end{array}$$

c
$$\begin{array}{r} \square\ 3\ 9\ \square \\ + 1\ \square\ 7\ 3 \\ \hline 9\ 2\ 6\ 7 \end{array}$$

d
$$\begin{array}{r} 5\ 3\ \square\ 5 \\ + 7\ \square\ 1\ \square \\ \hline 1\ \square\ 7\ 6\ 0 \end{array}$$

e
$$\begin{array}{r} 5\ 2\ 7\ 7 \\ + 8\ \square\ \square\ 4 \\ \hline 1\ \square\ 6\ 2\ \square \end{array}$$

f
$$\begin{array}{r} \square\ 3\ 2\ \square \\ + 5\ \square\ \square\ 5 \\ \hline 1\ 2\ 3\ 0\ 2 \end{array}$$

3 Total three of these numbers to make 20 000.
There are two different ways. Can you find them?

a $\boxed{} + \boxed{} + \boxed{} = 20\,000$

b $\boxed{} + \boxed{} + \boxed{} = 20\,000$

6934   7020   3224   8379   4601   4839   9842

Unit 16: Subtraction

Remember

When you **subtract** numbers that are too large to work out in your head, use a **written method**, like this.

730 becomes
600+130.
130−80=50

$$\begin{array}{r} 6\ ^13\ 1 \\ 3\not{7}\not{4}6 \\ -\ 1489 \\ \hline 2257 \end{array}$$

46 becomes
30+16.
16−9=7

Have a go

1 Answer each of these.

a	4725 − 2876	b	6230 − 4776	c	7060 − 3652	d	7832 − 2941	e	9400 − 6575

f	10314 − 3684	g	12319 − 8675	h	23425 − 12215	i	54196 − 18652	j	47105 − 29655

2 Write the missing numbers.

a
```
    □ 3 7 5
  −   2 □ 8 □
    4 3 8 8
```

b
```
    5 □ 6 □
  − 2 8 6 5
    2 1 □ 9
```

c
```
    □ □ 0 1
  −   3 6 4 □
    2 5 5 5
```

d
```
    1 0 □ 7 □
  −   □ 5 □ 5
    1 9 0 8
```

e
```
    □ 4 3 6 □
  −   7 □ □ 7
    2 6 6 8 4
```

f
```
    4 5 □ □ 4
  − 1 4 6 8 5
    3 □ 3 1 □
```

3 Join the pairs of numbers with a difference of 5555.

4735   11 200   10 290   6830

3845   9400   12 385   5645

Remember

Look at addition and subtraction problems carefully and work out the calculations you need.
Try to work out answers in your head using a mental method.
If the numbers are too difficult, use a written method.

Have a go

A darts game starts with a score of 501.
Players take turns to throw three darts. The total scored with the three darts is subtracted from the score. The first player to reach exactly zero is the winner.

Complete these charts and work out the winner.

a Fred's score

Throw	Dart score			Total	Score
	first	second	third		
					501
1	20	20	36	76	425
2	40	25	17		
3	38	60	10		
4	57	19	19		
5	60	36	9		
6	15	11	8		

b Joe's score

Throw	Dart score			Total	Score
	first	second	third		
					501
1	27	36	32	95	406
2	18	18	25		
3	26	60	20		
4	20	17	19		
5	15	20	16		
6	60	40	32		

The winner is _____

Unit 18: Decimal addition and subtraction

Remember

When you add or subtract decimals that are too large to work out in your head, use a written method, like this.

$$
\begin{array}{r}
23.93 \\
+\ 18.64 \\
\hline
42.57 \\
\tiny{1\ 1}
\end{array}
\qquad
\begin{array}{r}
\tiny{7\ 1} \\
6\cancel{8}.27 \\
-\ 43.54 \\
\hline
24.73
\end{array}
$$

Have a go

1 This table shows the scores of the top four gymnasts in a gymnastics event.

	Yalena	Beatrice	Nadia	Becky	Total
Vault	18.45	19.35	17.26	19.85	
Balance	19.23	18.69	19.36	18.68	
Bars	17.56	17.30	18.02	17.74	
Floor	19.80	19.24	19.38	18.97	
Total					

Complete the table to show:

a the total for each of the four events

b the totals for each of the four gymnasts.

2 Write the Gold, Silver and Bronze medal positions for the gymnasts.

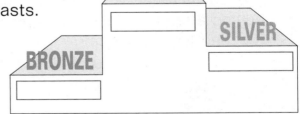

3 Use the table to answer these questions.

a How many more points in total did Becky score than Beatrice? _____

b How many more points were scored in total on the floor than the bars? _____

c Which two gymnasts had a difference in total score of 0.2? _____ and _____

d What is the difference between the highest and lowest individual scores on the vault? _____

Unit 19: Money calculations

Remember

When you **add** and **subtract money**, make sure that the columns are in line. The decimal points should be underneath each other.

You can check subtraction by addition.

$$
\begin{array}{r}
£37.08 \\
-\ £8.75 \\
\hline
£28.33 \\
\end{array}
$$

Check: £28.33 + £8.75 = £37.08

Have a go

1. Write the change you would get from £50 if you bought each pair of items.

a	b	c	d	e	f
£9.56	£18.08	£18.63	£7.86	£13.28	£13.85
£17.45	£12.43	£8.58	£36.29	£21.93	£32.96
Change £	Change £	Change £	Change £	Change £	Change £

2. Solve this problem.
   The Lewis family are thinking about buying a family membership ticket for their local museum.

Castle Museum

Admission prices
Adults £2.30
Children 85p
Annual family membership £45

How many times would they need to visit the museum for their family membership ticket to be cheaper than paying at each visit? ☐ times.

Unit 20: Mental multiplication

Remember

This is one way to work out 47 × 6 in your head:
Multiply the tens first, then the ones, and add the answers together.

40 × 6 = 240
7 × 6 = 42

So 47 × 6 = 240 + 42 = 282

Decimals can be worked out in the same way:

3.6 × 8
3 × 8 = 24
0.6 × 8 = 4.8

So 3.6 × 8 = 24 + 4.8 = 28.8

It is always a good idea to work out an **approximate** answer first.

Have a go

① Answer these.

a	b	c	d	e
30 × 4 =	50 × 8 =	60 × 3 =	90 × 2 =	70 × 6 =
38 × 4 =	57 × 8 =	64 × 3 =	93 × 2 =	74 × 6 =

②
a	b	c	d	e
79 × 3 =	84 × 6 =	95 × 4 =	47 × 8 =	63 × 9 =

③ Calculate the area of these rectangles.

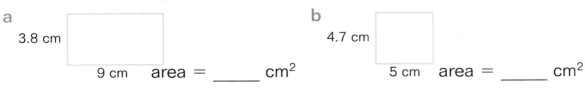

a
3.8 cm
9 cm   area = _____ cm²

b
4.7 cm
5 cm   area = _____ cm²

c
6.8 cm
3 cm   area = _____ cm²

d
9.2 cm
8 cm   area = _____ cm²

Unit 21: Written multiplication

Remember

If you need to multiply together two numbers that are too difficult to work out in your head, try using the **grid method**.

Example: 58 × 73

1. Write them in a grid, breaking up each number into tens and units.

2. Multiply each pair of numbers to complete the grid.

3. Add up the rows in the grid.

4. Add up the two totals.

It is always a good idea to work out an **approximate answer** first.

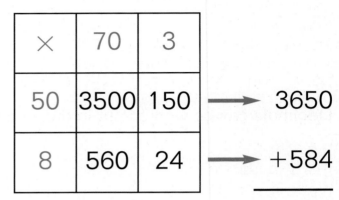

×	70	3
50	3500	150
8	560	24

3500 + 150 → 3650

560 + 24 → +584

4234

Have a go

1. Use the grid method to answer these.

a
×	50	3
60		
8		

b
×	50	3
80		
6		

c
×	60	4
70		
2		

d
×	30	8
50		
9		

e
×	80	2
40		
6		

f
×	30	9
70		
4		

2. Calculate the cost of each set of stamps.

a 25 ×  34p stamps ➡ £_____

b 18 × 67p stamps ➡ £_____

c 29 × 45p stamps ➡ £_____

d 32 × 73p stamps ➡ £_____

Unit 22: Division with remainders

Remember

There are different ways of dividing numbers. Whichever way you choose it is always a good idea to work out an **approximate** answer first.

$387 \div 4$ is approximately $400 \div 4$, so the answer will be a bit less than 100.

```
        9 6 r 3
    4 ) 3 8 7
      − 3 6 0   (4 × 90)
          2 7
        − 2 4   (4 × 6)
            3
```

```
        9 6 r 3
    4 ) 3 8₂7
```

Have a go

1 Use your own method to answer these.

a $245 \div 3 =$ _____   b $386 \div 5 =$ _____   c $189 \div 4 =$ _____

d $522 \div 6 =$ _____   e $367 \div 5 =$ _____   f $412 \div 8 =$ _____

g $308 \div 9 =$ _____   h $529 \div 4 =$ _____   i $488 \div 3 =$ _____

2 Look at these numbers.

(116) (677) (780) (425) (762)

> Tip: Some answers may have more than one number.

Which of them:

a divide exactly by 4   ⟶ _____

b divide exactly by 5   ⟶ _____

c divide exactly by 6   ⟶ _____

d leave a remainder of 1 when divided by 4 ⟶ _____

e leave a remainder of 2 when divided by 5 ⟶ _____

f leave a remainder of 2 when divided by 3 ⟶ _____

3 Write the missing digits 1 to 4.

a
```
        7 ▢
    3 ) 2 ▢ 6
```

b
```
          8 3
    ▢ ) 3 ▢ 2
```

[1]   [3]

[2]   [4]

Unit 23: Division — decimal answers

 **Remember**

A **quotient** is an answer to a division. Sometimes quotients can be written with decimal answers.

134 ÷ 5
134 = 134.0 = 134.00
There can be any number of zeros after the decimal point.

$$\begin{array}{r} 26.8 \\ 5\overline{)134.00} \\ {}_{34} \end{array}$$

Make sure that you line up the decimal points.

143 ÷ 3
Some decimal quotients do not work out exactly: they go on and on as a recurring decimal.

$$\begin{array}{r} 47.6666 \\ 3\overline{)143.0000} \\ {}_{22\ 222} \end{array}$$

This is 47.67 rounded to **two decimal places**.

 **Have a go**

1 Answer these using decimals.

a
5)193

b
8)276

c
4)435

d
5)307

e
5)411

f
2)319

g
8)285

h
4)639

2 Answer these, rounding the answer to two decimal places.

a
3)130

b
6)295

c
7)178

d
9)769

e
6)283

f
3)614

g
9)379

h
7)408

3 Write the missing digits 1 to 6.   1   2   3   4   5   6

a
$$\begin{array}{r} 7\ \square\ .\ \square\ 5 \\ 8\overline{)58\ \square} \end{array}$$

b
$$\begin{array}{r} 5\ 4\ .\ 7\ \square \\ \square\overline{)2\ \square\ 9} \end{array}$$

Unit 24: Money problems

Remember

When you multiply and divide money amounts, estimate an approximate answer first. If you can't work out the answer in your head, try these methods.

Method 1
What is £7.39 × 5?
This is approximately £7 × 5, which is £35

Method 2
What is £3.36 ÷ 4?
This is approximately £3 divided by 4, which is 75p

Have a go

1 Calculate the total cost of each of these.

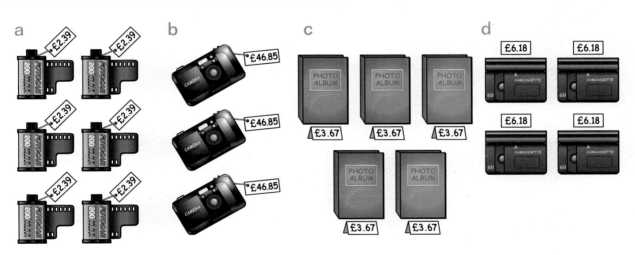

a   b   c   d

£2.39 £2.39 £2.39 £2.39 £2.39 £2.39

£46.85 £46.85 £46.85

£3.67 £3.67 £3.67 £3.67 £3.67

£6.18 £6.18 £6.18 £6.18

Total: £_____   Total: £_____   Total: £_____   Total: £_____

2 Calculate the cost of one of each of these.

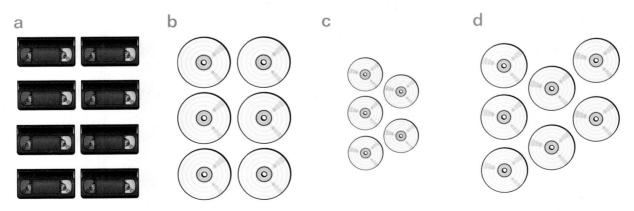

a   b   c   d

Total price: £22.08   Total price: £55.44   Total price: £11.95   Total price: £62.72
Cost of each item: Cost of each item: Cost of each item: Cost of each item:

£_____   £_____   £_____   £_____

Unit 25: 2D shapes – quadrilaterals

Remember

Quadrilaterals are shapes with four straight sides.
Some quadrilaterals have special names and properties:

Square: 4 equal sides, 4 equal/right angles

Rectangle: 2 pairs of equal sides, 4 equal/right angles.

Rhombus: 4 equal sides, opposite angles equal, opposite sides parallel

Parallelogram: Opposite sides equal and parallel

Trapezium: One pair of parallel sides of different lengths

Kite: Adjacent sides equal, one pair of opposite angles equal.

Have a go

1 Name each shape. Tick any right angles.

a

b

c

d

e

f

g

h

2 Draw three different quadrilaterals on this grid. Use a ruler and draw them as carefully as you can.

Unit 26: 2D shapes – polygons

Remember

Polygons are straight-sided closed shapes.
The sides of a **regular polygon** are all the same length and all the angles are the same size.

This is a regular pentagon.	This is not a regular pentagon.	These are not polygons.

Have a go

Complete this table of polygons.

shape	sketch	number of sides	number of right angles	number of lines of symmetry
rectangle				
equilateral triangle				
rhombus				
isosceles triangle				
regular hexagon				
square				
kite				
parallelogram				

Unit 27: 3D solids

Remember

Don't confuse prisms and pyramids.

Prisms
The shape of the end gives the prism its name.
Cuboids and cubes are special types of prisms.

Pyramids
The shape of the base gives the pyramid its name.
The sides of a pyramid are always triangular.

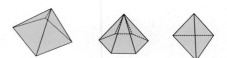

Have a go

① Sort these shapes into prisms and pyramids.

Tick the correct boxes.

Shape	a	b	c	d	e	f	g	h
Prism								
Pyramid								

② Draw lines from each shape to the correct parts of this Venn diagram.

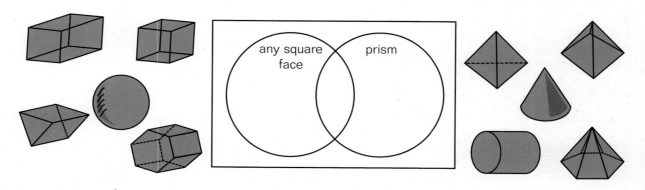

any square face   prism

32

Unit 28: Nets of 3D solids

Remember

The **net** of a solid is what it looks like when it is opened out flat. You can find the net of a box by carefully pulling open a cardboard box so that it is flat.

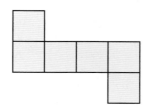

Have a go

1 Write the names of each of these solids from their nets.

a
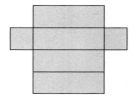
_____

b
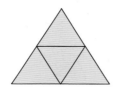
_____

c
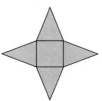
_____

d
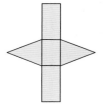
_____

e
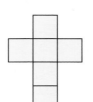
_____

f

_____

2 On this page there are two nets of cubes. Draw three different nets of cubes on this grid.

Unit 29: Angles and lines

Remember

There are rules for working out angles:

Angles in a straight line add up to 180°.

150° 30°

Angles around a point add up to 360°.

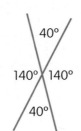

40°
140° 140°
40°

Angles of a triangle add up to 180°.

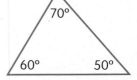

70°
60° 50°

Have a go

1 Work out the size of the missing angles for these triangles.

a
55° 60°
_____°

b
65°
90°
_____°

c
70° 70°
_____°

d
64° 48°
_____°

e
90°
34°
_____°

f
43°
112°
_____°

g
105°
54°
_____°

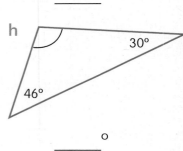

h
30°
46°
_____°

2 Work out the missing angles on these lines.

a
38° ☐°

b
☐° 152°

c
☐° 90°

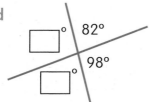

d
☐° 82°
98°
☐°

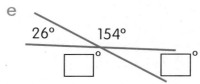

e
26° 154°
☐° ☐°

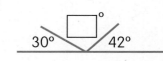

f
☐°
30° 42°

34

Unit 30: Symmetry

Remember

Shapes are **symmetrical** if both sides match when a **mirror line** or a **line of symmetry** is drawn. Some shapes have more than one line of symmetry.

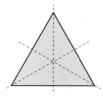

3 lines of symmetry

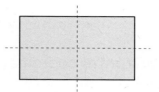

2 lines of symmetry

Have a go

1. Draw the lines of symmetry on each of these shapes.

   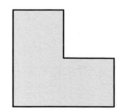   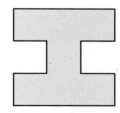

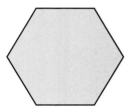      

2. Colour these pentagons in different ways to make symmetrical designs.

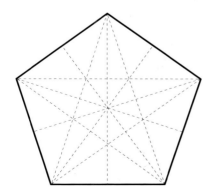   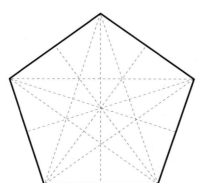   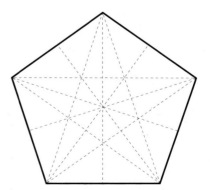

Unit 31: Coordinates

Remember

A **coordinate** is a position on a grid.
Negative numbers can be used to
show positions.
The coordinates of A are (−3, 4)
The coordinates of B are (3, 5)
Read the **horizontal** coordinate first
and then the **vertical** coordinate.

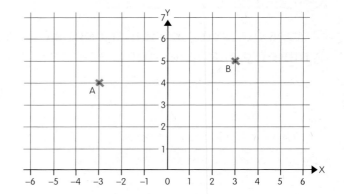

Have a go

1. Draw two triangles at the following points:

Triangle 1
(−7, 3) (−6, 7) (−3, 2)

Triangle 2
(0, 2) (4, 7) (6, 1)

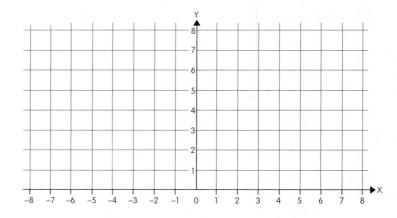

2. The graph shows two corners of a quadrilateral.

   a What are the coordinates of:

   Position A ⟶ _____

   Position B ⟶ _____

   b Plot the positions of the
   other two corners and
   draw the shape.
   The coordinates are:

   Position C ⟶ (−6, 6)

   Position D ⟶ (2, 2)

   Name the shape: _____

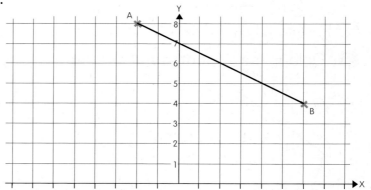

Unit 32: Reflection

Remember

A **line of symmetry** is the same as a mirror line.
One side of the line is the reflection of the other side.

These two shapes are a reflection of each other.

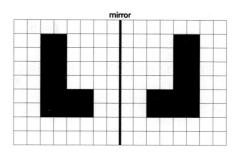

Have a go

1 Draw the reflection of the triangle.

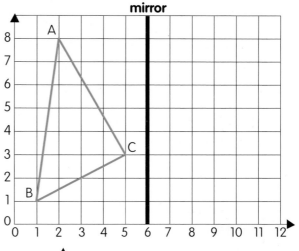

2 Plot these coordinates on the grid.

A (5, 7) B (8, 8) C (5, 5) D (2, 8)

- Join them in order to make a quadrilateral
- Draw the reflection of the quadrilateral
- Write the coordinates of the reflected quadrilateral

(__, __) (__, __) (__, __) (__, __)

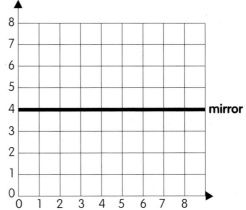

3 Draw a reflection of this pentagon.

- Write the coordinates of the reflected pentagon.

(__, __) (__, __) (__, __) (__, __) (__, __)

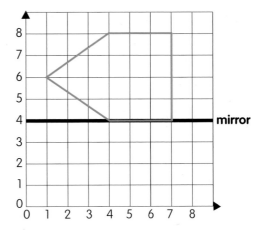

Unit 33: Measures

Length, **weight** (or **mass**) and **capacity** are all measured using different units.

<u>Length</u>
1 centimetre (cm) = 10 millimetres (mm)
1 metre (m) = 100 cm
1 kilometre (km) = 1000 m

<u>Weight</u>
1 kilogram (kg) = 1000 grams (g)
1 tonne = 1000 kg

<u>Capacity</u>
1 litre (l) = 1000 millilitres (ml)
1 centilitre (cl) = 10 ml

You use **decimals** and **fractions** to show parts of amounts. For example:
$25 \text{ cm} = \frac{1}{4} \text{ m}$
500 g = 0.5 kg
10 ml = 0.01 litre

 **Have a go**

1 Complete these measures.

a $3\frac{1}{2}$ m = _____ cm

b 1.9 kg = _____ g

c 14.2 cm = _____ mm

d 0.25 l = _____ ml

e 2.75 km = _____ m

f 0.6 kg = _____ g

g $4\frac{3}{4}$ l = _____ ml

h 7.3 km = _____ m

2 Put in <, > or = to make each statement true.

a 6.5 cm ____ 650 mm

b 6400 g ____ $6\frac{1}{4}$ kg

c 2300 ml ____ 2.3 litre

d 82 mm ____ $8\frac{1}{2}$ cm

e 3.8 km ____ 3750 m

f 0.5 kg ____ 50 g

g 5.6 l ____ 5060 ml

h 580 cm ____ 5.8 m

Unit 34: Area and perimeter

Remember

You can find the **area of a rectangle** by using a **formula**.

Area = length × width
  A = l × w

The **perimeter of a rectangle** can be calculated using this **formula**:

Perimeter = 2 × (length + width)
  P = 2(l + w)

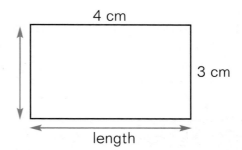

Area = 4 cm × 3 cm = 12 cm²   Perimeter = 2 × (4 cm + 3 cm) = 14 cm

Have a go

① Use the formulae to calculate the area and perimeter of each of these.

a
4 cm   7 cm

area = ___ cm² perimeter = ___ cm

b
6 cm   9 cm

area = ___ cm² perimeter = ___ cm

c
4 cm   5 cm

area = ___ cm² perimeter = ___ cm

d
3 cm   8 cm

area = ___ cm² perimeter = ___ cm

② Answer these problems.

a The length of one of the sides of a square is 6 cm.
  What is its perimeter and area?   Perimeter = ____ Area = ____

b The area of a square is 81 cm². What is its perimeter? Perimeter = ____

c The perimeter of a square is 48 cm. What is its area?   Area = ____

Unit 35: Area – compound shapes

Remember

To find the area of **compound shapes**, split them into rectangles.

Area of a rectangle = length × width

A = l × w

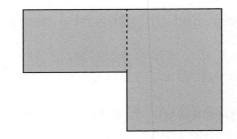

Have a go

Calculate the area of these shapes.

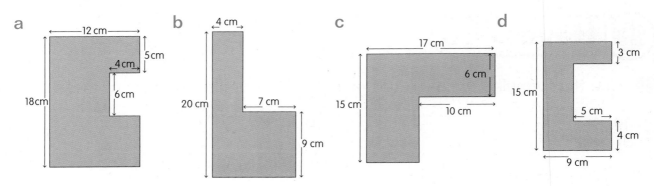

a 12 cm 5 cm 4 cm 6 cm 18 cm

Area = _____

b 4 cm 20 cm 7 cm 9 cm

Area = _____

c 17 cm 6 cm 15 cm 10 cm

Area = _____

d 3 cm 15 cm 5 cm 4 cm 9 cm

Area = _____

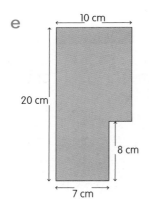

e 10 cm 20 cm 8 cm 7 cm

Area = _____

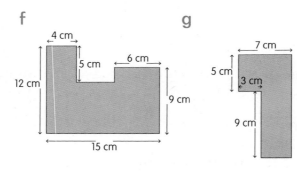

f 4 cm 5 cm 6 cm 12 cm 9 cm 15 cm

Area = _____

g 7 cm 5 cm 3 cm 9 cm

Area = _____

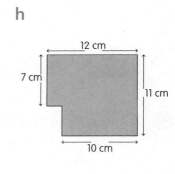

h 12 cm 7 cm 11 cm 10 cm

Area = _____

Unit 36: Volume

Remember

Volume of a cuboid = area of the base × height

Area of base = length × width = 5 cm × 2 cm
Volume of cuboid = 5 cm × 2 cm × 4 cm = 40 cm³
Don't forget to use cm³.

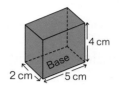

Have a go

1 Calculate the volumes of the following cuboids.

a [cm³]
10 cm, 8 cm, 6 cm

b [cm³]
3 cm, 6 cm, 4 cm

c [cm³]
2 cm, 9 cm, 5 cm

d [cm³]
3 cm, 4 cm, 5 cm

e [cm³]
4 cm, 4 cm, 2 cm

f [cm³]
5 cm, 10 cm, 5 cm

g [cm³]
3 cm, 2 cm, 8 cm

h [cm³]
7 cm, 7 cm, 10 cm

2 Complete this table.

length	width	height	volume
8 cm	4 cm	3 cm	
5 cm	2 cm		60 cm³
	9 cm	4 cm	360 cm³
8 cm		2 cm	48 cm³
4 cm	3 cm	7 cm	
10 cm	6 cm		180 cm³

Unit 37: Time

Remember

a.m. stands for *ante meridiem*, which is in the morning.
p.m. stands for *post meridiem*, which is in the afternoon.

Timetables and digital watches often use the **24-hour clock**. The 24-hour clock uses four digits.
8.35 a.m. is written as 08:35
8.35 p.m. is written as 20:35

Have a go

1 Write these using the 24-hour clock.

   a 7.20 a.m. ⬚   b 4.15 p.m. ⬚   c 9.05 p.m. ⬚

   d 11.30 a.m. ⬚   e 1.40 p.m. ⬚   f 2.53 p.m. ⬚

   g 6.03 a.m. ⬚   h 3.48 p.m. ⬚   i 10.41 a.m. ⬚

2 Write these using a.m. and p.m.

   a 14:55 ⬚   b 17:20 ⬚   c 02:05 ⬚

   d 11:40 ⬚   e 13:25 ⬚   f 06:14 ⬚

   g 21:53 ⬚   h 10:28 ⬚   i 15:04 ⬚

3 Draw hands to show the times.

   a 18:55    b 19:40    c 11:35

   d 22:05    e 14:20    f 07:50

Unit 38: Timetables

Remember

Timetables and digital watches often use the **24-hour clock**.
If you need to find out how long a journey is, count on along a time line.
Example: A train leaves at 13:45 and arrives at 16:05. How long is the journey?

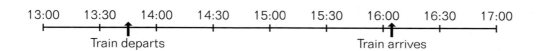

15 mins + 2 hrs + 5 mins = 2 hrs 20 mins

Have a go

Use this timetable to answer these questions.

	Train 1	Train 2	Train 3	Train 4	Train 5
London King's Cross	15:10	15:30	15:40	16:00	16:10
Peterborough	15:54	16:14	16:31	....	16:55
Grantham	16:13	....	....	....	17:15
Doncaster	16:56	17:03	17:21	....	17:52
Wakefield	17:14	....	17:39	....	18:13
Leeds	17:35	....	17:57	....	18:35
York	....	17:26	....	17:49	....
Darlington	....	17:59	....	18:18	....
Durham	....	18:17	....	....	....
Newcastle	....	18:35	....	18:48	....

a What time does the 15:30 from King's Cross arrive in York? _____

b Which is the fastest train from King's Cross to Doncaster? _____

c How many stations are stopped at on the 16:10 from King's Cross before arriving at Leeds? _____

d How long does it take the 16:14 from Peterborough to reach Newcastle?

_____

e The 15:10 from King's Cross is running 18 minutes late into Doncaster. What time will it arrive? _____

f If you catch the 16:00 from King's Cross and have been on the train for a little over two hours, what is the next station you will arrive at?

_____

g How long does it take the 15:40 from King's Cross to reach Leeds?

_____

h You arrive at Peterborough station at 4 o'clock to catch a train to Wakefield. How long will it be until you arrive at Wakefield? _____

Unit 39: Data – line graphs

Line graphs have points plotted which are then joined with a line. There are many different types, but for all of them you must read them carefully:

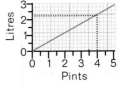

- go up from the **horizontal** axis to meet the line or point
- from this point go across to the **vertical** axis to give the value.

4 pints is approximately $2\frac{1}{2}$ litres

① Temperature is measured in degrees – Fahrenheit (°F) and Celsius (°C).

This graph converts °F to °C (approximately).

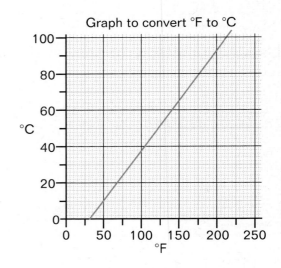

Use the graph to complete this table.

°F	50		150		65		90	
°C		80		25		30		42

② This shows the average monthly temperature for Nice in France.

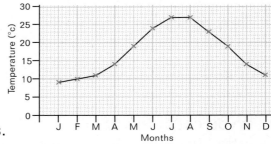

Use the graph to answer these questions.

a What was the average temperature in May? _____

b In which month was the average temperature 23 °C? _____

c What was the difference between the hottest and coldest months? _____

d Which month had the same average as March? _____

e Which month was 5 °C warmer than October? _____

Unit 40: Data – averages

Remember

There are three types of **average**.

Example: What is the average of this set of numbers? | 6   9   4   7   9 |

Mode	Median	Mean
The mode is the number that occurs the most often. 9 is the mode for the set of numbers shown above.	The median is the middle number. To work out the median: • Put the numbers in ascending order 4, 6, 7, 9, 9 • The middle number, 7, is the median.	The mean is: total ÷ number of items. 6 + 9 + 4 + 7 + 9 = 35 There are five numbers. 35 ÷ 5 = 7 The mean is 7.

Have a go

1 Here are the costs of seven pairs of sunglasses.

  a Write the prices in order, starting with the lowest:

  | £ | | £ | | £ | | £ | | £ | | £ | | £ | |

  b Which price is the mode? | £ |

  c Which is the median price? | £ |

  d Calculate the mean price. | £ |

2 This table shows the temperature during a sunny week in Spain.

  a Write the temperatures in order, starting with the lowest:

  b Which temperature is the mode?

  c Which is the median temperature?

  d Calculate the mean temperature.

Spanish weather during one week		
Mon	78°	○
Tues	80°	○
Wed	79°	○
Thurs	81°	○
Fri	81°	○
Sat	80°	○
Sun	81°	○

Test 1

Check how much you have learned.

Answer the questions.
Mark your answers. Fill in your scores.

SCORE

1 Write the value of each number.

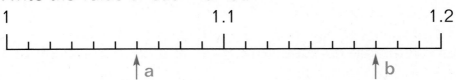

1   1.1   1.2

↑a   ↑b

a [ ]   b [ ]

out of 2

2 Write the missing numbers in this sequence.

| 17 | 9 | | | −15 | −23 | |

out of 1

3 Complete these measures.

a 145 mm = _____ cm   b 2650 g = _____ kg

c 525 cm = _____ m   d 6200 ml = _____ l

out of 4

4 This graph shows the conversion between euros and pounds sterling.

1 euro = 60p
What is the approximate value of:

a €4.00 ➡ _____

b £6.00 ➡ _____

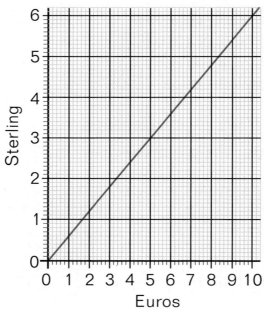

out of 2

5 Write the missing numbers.

a $39 + \boxed{} = 47$

b $\boxed{} - 8 = 54$

c $70 + \boxed{} = 130$

out of 3

6 Complete these equivalent fractions.

$$\frac{2}{\bigcirc} = \frac{\bigcirc}{30} = \frac{6}{9} = \frac{14}{\bigcirc} = \frac{\bigcirc}{45}$$

out of 1

7 Join the names to the correct shapes.

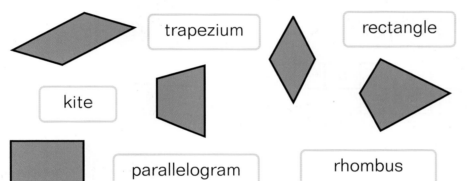

trapezium

rectangle

kite

parallelogram

rhombus

out of 1

8 Convert these times.

12-hour	24-hour
7.25 a.m.	
	19:50
3.32 p.m.	
	10:39

out of 1

9 Work out the total.

```
  8408
+ 2355
+ 3294
───────
```

out of 1

out of 1

10 What is 4255 less than 9105? $\boxed{}$

out of 1

Total out of 17

Test 2

Check how much you have learned.

Answer the questions.
Mark your answers. Fill in your scores.

1 Write these numbers in order, starting with the smallest.

29.35, 29.05, 25.9, 29.29, 29.5

out of 1

2 Write the function and complete the table of results.

IN	0	1	2	3	4	5	6
OUT	−5	−2	1	4	7		

out of 2

3 What is the volume of this cuboid?

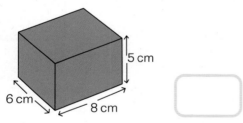

5 cm
6 cm
8 cm

out of 1

4 These are the costs of five canned foods.

 48p 39p 39p 42p 32p

a Which price is the mode? _____

b Which is the median price? _____

c What is the mean price? _____

out of 3

5 Answer these.

a $19 - (3 \times 6) =$

out of 2

b $(7 \times 5) - (16 + 9) =$

6 Write these fractions in order of size, starting from the smallest.

$\frac{5}{6}$ $\frac{2}{3}$ $\frac{4}{5}$ $\frac{1}{2}$ $\frac{7}{10}$

out of 1

7 Ring the polygons.
Tick the regular polygons.

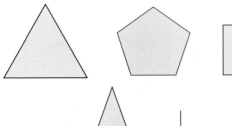

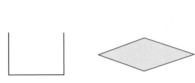

out of 2

8 Answer these questions about this bus timetable.

Bus Station	13:20	14:11
High Street	13:39	14:29
Hospital	13:56	....
Leisure Centre	14:15	14:46
Hope Lane	14:21	....
Barons Field	14:37	14:58

a How long is the journey from the hospital to the Leisure Centre? _____

b What is the total journey time if you catch the 14:11 bus from the Bus Station to Barons Field? _____

out of 2

9 Work out the totals.

a
```
    4.93
+  31.09
_____
```

b
```
   174.90
+  87.68
_____
```

out of 2

10 Answer each of these.

a
```
   47.03
-  29.45
_____
```

b
```
   108.39
-  84.67
_____
```

out of 2

Total out of 18

Test 3

Check how much you have learned.

Answer the questions.
Mark your answers. Fill in your scores.

1 Circle the numbers that are multiples of both 3 and 4.

423   256   144   276   524   216

out of 1

2 What are the perimeter and area of this rectangle?

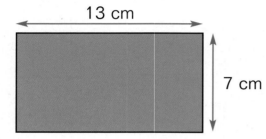

13 cm

7 cm

perimeter = ☐ cm

area = ☐ cm²

out of 2

3 Answer these.

a 76 × 4 = ☐   b 5.4 × 8 = ☐

out of 2

4 Use your own method to answer these.

a 364 ÷ 5 = ☐   b 831 ÷ 6 = ☐

out of 2

5 Tick the odd one out in each set.

a

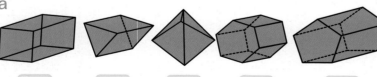

☐ ☐ ☐ ☐ ☐ ☐

b

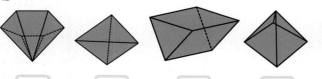

☐ ☐ ☐ ☐ ☐ ☐

out of 2

50

6 What are the coordinates of A and B?

A ⟶ _____   B ⟶ _____

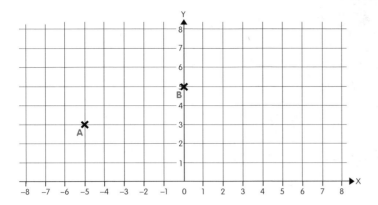

7 Write the decimals and equivalent fractions.

a $\dfrac{3}{5}$ =

b — = 0.25

c $\dfrac{7}{10}$ =

d — = 0.02

out of 4

8 Change these fractions to percentages.

a $\dfrac{3}{5}$ = ☐ %   b $\dfrac{7}{20}$ = ☐ %   c $\dfrac{39}{50}$ = ☐ %

out of 3

9 Draw a reflection of the shape.

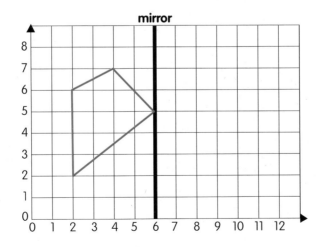

out of 1

10 Liam bought three postcards and two posters from a gift shop.

What change did he get from £20?

_____

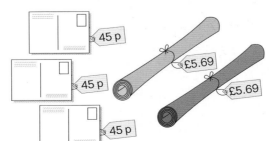

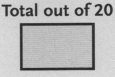

out of 1

Total out of 20

Test 4

Check how much you have learned.

Answer the questions.
Mark your answers. Fill in your scores.

1 Write all the pairs of factors of each of these.

a 45
(__ , __)
(__ , __)
(__ , __)

b 30
(__ , __)
(__ , __)
(__ , __)
(__ , __)

out of 2

2 Calculate the area of this shape.

_____

out of 1

3 Answer these.

a 34 × 53

×	30	4
50			→
3			→

_____

b 39 × 78

×	30	9
70			→
8			→

_____

out of 2

4 Answer these using decimals.

a
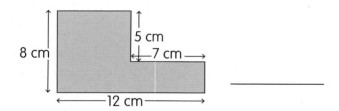
5) 3 8 2

b

8) 4 9 5

out of 2

5 Write the names of each of these solids from their nets.

a
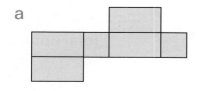

_____

b
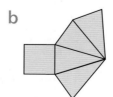

_____

out of 2

6 What are the coordinates of A and B?

A ➡ (__,__)   B ➡ (__,__)

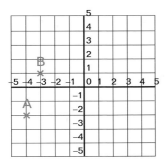

out of 2

7 Write the answers.

a 13.85 × 10 = _____   b 0.762 × 100 = _____

c 14.9 ÷ 10 = _____   d 70 ÷ 100 = _____

out of 4

8 Calculate the percentages of these amounts.

a £3.60

10% ➡ _____
20% ➡ _____
5% ➡ _____

b £2.40

10% ➡ _____
30% ➡ _____
15% ➡ _____

out of 2

9 Draw the lines of symmetry on this shape.

out of 1

10 Answer these.

a Three notebooks cost £3.75.

What would one notebook cost? _____

b Pens cost £4.93 per set.

What would six sets cost? _____

out of 2

Total out of 20

Parents' notes

Unit 1: Decimal numbers   The place value is the position or place of a digit in a number. The same digit has a different value at different places in the number, on either side of the decimal point. Your child needs to know the value of the decimal places: tenths, hundredths and thousandths. Relate these to fractions and that will help him or her see how small these decimals are. A common error is to think that, for example, 0.2 is smaller than 0.18. Your child should see that $\frac{2}{10}$ $(= \frac{20}{100})$ is bigger than $\frac{18}{100}$.

Unit 2: Decimals – place value   The same digit has a different value at different places in a number, and this includes decimal numbers. When you multiply a number by 10, all the digits move one place to the left and a zero is put at the end of the number. When you divide a number by 10, all the digits move one place to the right. The important thing is that the decimal point stays where it is – it is the digits that move.

Unit 3: Ordering numbers   Your child needs to know the value of the decimal places: tenths, hundredths and thousandths. Relate these to fractions, and that will help your child see how small these decimals are. Comparing and ordering decimals is easier when they are lined up vertically. Each decimal place can then be compared. A common error is to think that, for example, 0.2 is smaller than 0.18. Your child needs to see that $\frac{2}{10}$ $(= \frac{20}{100})$ is bigger than $\frac{18}{100}$.

Unit 4: Number sequences   Number sequences are lists of numbers with a pattern between each number. Encourage your child to work out the difference between each number, as that gives the rule for the missing numbers. If negative numbers are involved, make sure that zero is included in the sequences.

Unit 5: Function machines   A function is a rule for changing one set of numbers into another set. A function machine can show functions by having numbers going into the machine, following the rule or function, and coming out of the machine. Single operations, such as × 4 or + 5 are fairly easy to see from the numbers, but two-stage operations such as × 2 + 3 are more difficult. Carry out the operations in order to work out the numbers coming out. To work out the function from numbers coming in and out of a machine, look at the relationship between each pair of numbers and try to work out the rule for changing each of them.

Unit 6: Multiples   Your child needs to recognise multiples of different numbers to 10. Make sure that he or she understands that multiples don't stop at 10 × a number, but go on and on. The important thing is to recognise the 'rule' for a set of multiples. These are called 'rules of divisibility', used to recognise whether a large number can be divided by, or is a multiple of, a certain number. For example, we know that 717 is a multiple of 3 because the digits total 15, which is a multiple of 3.

Unit 7: Factors   A factor of a whole number is any whole number that divides exactly into it. It helps to write factors in pairs and makes it easier to see if you've included them all: factors of 30 ➡ (1, 30) (2, 15) (3, 10) (5, 6). The number 1 and the number itself are always factors of a number. If a number has only these two factors, it is called a prime number. Note that 1 is not a prime number as it only has one factor: 1. A number always has an even number of factors, unless it is a square number. For example, 16, being a square number, has five factors: 1, 2, 4, 8 and 16.

Unit 8: Fractions   Equivalence in fractions (such as $\frac{2}{3} = \frac{8}{12}$) is a very important concept for your child to understand. Check that your child knows that the number above the line of a fraction is the numerator and the number below the line is the denominator. Look for the pattern between equivalent fractions. For example, $\frac{2}{3}$ $= \frac{8}{12}$. Compare the denominators and numerators and you can see that 2 × 4 = 8 and 3 × 4 = 12. Simplifying a fraction is making a fraction as simple as possible. So $\frac{4}{20}$ can be simplified to $\frac{1}{5}$.

Unit 9: Ordering fractions   Equivalence in fractions (such as $\frac{2}{3} = \frac{8}{12}$) is a very important concept for your child to understand. Check that he or she knows that the number above the line of a fraction is the numerator and the number below is the denominator. To put fractions in order of size, it is usually necessary to make all the denominators the same. This is done by turning them into equivalent fractions with the same denominator. For example, to show that $\frac{2}{3}$ is larger than $\frac{3}{5}$, turn them both into fifteenths: $\frac{2}{3}$ is $\frac{10}{15}$ and $\frac{3}{5}$ is $\frac{9}{15}$, so $\frac{2}{3}$ is larger than $\frac{3}{5}$.

Unit 10: Fractions and decimals   Fractions and decimals are the same thing but written in different ways – they are parts of a whole number. It is useful to be able to change fractions to decimals and the other way round. Encourage your child to learn all the tenths, so that he or she knows, for example, that $\frac{3}{10}$ is 0.3. Your child can then work out fifths – for example, $\frac{2}{5}$ is $\frac{4}{10}$ which is 0.4. When converting fractions to decimals, the line in a fraction means 'divided by'. So, written as a division: $\frac{3}{8} = 3 \div 8 = 0.375$.

Unit 11: Percentages   Percentages are simply fractions out of 100. Your child needs to understand equivalent fractions (e.g. $\frac{20}{100} = \frac{1}{5}$) in order to convert fractions to percentages and vice versa. To change fractions to percentages, make them out of 100 – for example $\frac{11}{20}$ as a percentage is 55% (multiply numerator and denominator by 5). To change percentages to fractions, write the percentage as a fraction out of 100 and then simplify. For example, 80% or $\frac{80}{100}$ is the same as $\frac{4}{5}$ (divide numerator and denominator by 20).

Unit 12: Percentages of amounts   Percentages are simply fractions out of 100. For working out percentages of amounts, two methods have been shown. To change percentages to fractions, write the percentage as a fraction out of 100 and then simplify. For example, 20% or $\frac{20}{100}$ is the same as $\frac{1}{5}$. So 20% of £30 is $\frac{1}{5}$ of £30, which is £6. A good alternative method is to use 10% to help work it out: 10% of £30 is £3, so 20% is double that, which is £6.

Unit 13: Number facts   Your child needs to be able to recall quickly all the addition and subtraction facts up to 20. Once your child knows these, he or she can use them to work out other facts based on them. So, for example, once your child knows that $8 + 6 = 14$, he or she should be able to work out $80 + 60$, $18 + 6$, $38 + 6$, $800 + 600$, and so on.

Unit 14: Brackets   Brackets in a calculation show that the part of the calculation in the brackets needs to be worked out first. Compare calculations with brackets in different places and try to think of real problems that would need to be worked out in different orders.

Unit 15: Addition   When adding two numbers, always encourage your child to look at the numbers first to see if they can be added mentally. If the numbers are too big, then your child will need to use a written method. There are several different written methods, and the 'vertical' method covered in this unit is just one example. It may be that your child wants to make informal jottings of numbers as they are added, or use the formal method shown. Go through each step carefully, making sure that the columns are lined up.

Unit 16: Subtraction   As with addition, always encourage your child to look at the numbers first to see if they can be subtracted mentally. If your child needs to use a written method, he or she can choose between the formal method shown or an alternative. The 'vertical' method is called decomposition, where tens and hundreds are exchanged to make the numbers easier to work with. An alternative is to find the difference between two numbers, counting on from the smaller number to the next ten and then on to the larger number. This is a more informal written method, similar to the mental method of counting on.

Unit 17: Addition and subtraction   When adding several numbers or subtracting numbers, always encourage your child to look at the numbers first to see if they can be calculated mentally. If the numbers are too complicated, then your child will need to use a written method. There are several different written methods, including formal 'vertical' methods or informal jottings of numbers. Encourage your child to explain the strategies or methods he or she is using to complete the charts.

Unit 18: Decimal addition and subtraction   With both addition and subtraction always encourage your child to look at the numbers first to see if they can be calculated mentally. If they need to use a written method, they can choose between the formal method shown or their own method. The 'vertical' method of subtraction is called decomposition, where numbers are 'exchanged' to make them easier to work with. For both the vertical methods for addition and subtraction, make sure that the decimal points are lined up and work out a quick approximate answer first.

Unit 19: Money calculations   When adding money amounts that are difficult to do mentally, make sure that the columns line up so that the decimal points are under each other. Then the normal written method for addition can be used. With subtraction or working out change, it may be easier to use a 'shopkeeper's method', even as a written method. This involves counting on from the cost of the item to the amount given, writing down the money amounts as you go along, and totalling the amount of change.

Unit 20: Mental multiplication   The most popular method of multiplying a two-digit number by a single digit is to break up (partition) the two-digit number. So, for example, 36×5 is 30×5 (150) added to 6×5 (30). So, 36×5 is 180. This can be done in any order – tens first or ones first. It is exactly the same when multiplying decimals, breaking them up into whole numbers and decimals and multiplying each part.

Unit 21: Written multiplication   Multiplying with large numbers is tricky to do in your head, but this grid method works well on paper. It involves breaking numbers up and multiplying each part. Go through each of the four stages carefully, making sure that your child understands the method. Practise so that it becomes a quick and accurate method, and a good alternative to the written vertical method.

Unit 22: Division with remainders   Written division methods are quite tricky, so it is important that your child is confident at dividing numbers mentally and knows the multiplication tables. This will help speed up the stages of working out a written division and allow your child to concentrate on the process. Encourage your child to estimate an approximate answer first. Read through the long method where the number to be divided is broken up into hundreds, tens and ones, and then relate this to the short method. The long method will probably be the method that your child will want to use when carrying out written division calculations.

Unit 23: Division – decimal answers   Written division methods are quite tricky, so it is important that your child is confident at dividing numbers mentally and knows the multiplication tables. This will help speed up the stages of working out a written division and allow him or her to concentrate on the process. Encourage your child to estimate an approximate answer first. Make sure that the decimal points are lined up and, if necessary, round the decimal answer to two or three decimal places.

Unit 24: Money problems   When multiplying and dividing money amounts that are difficult to do mentally, make sure that your child estimates an approximate answer first. Ask your child to explain the methods while working them out. If it is causing your child difficulties, ask if he or she has any other strategies that could be tried.

Unit 25: 2D shapes – quadrilaterals   Any shape with four straight sides is a quadrilateral. There are many specially named quadrilaterals with certain features. Look at the properties of the different shapes and try to recognise what makes, for example, a rhombus unique. Make sure that your child recognises that some shapes may have more than one name. For example, a square is a special rectangle and also a type of parallelogram.

Unit 26: 2D shapes – polygons   Polygons are two-dimensional shapes with straight sides. Each has a special name related to the number of sides, so, for example, any shape with six straight sides is a hexagon. Look at the properties of the different shapes and try to recognise what makes, for example, a rhombus unique. Make sure that your child recognises regular polygons, with equal length sides and equal angles.

Unit 27: 3D solids   Your child will need to be able to recognise and name 3D solids and describe their properties. This will involve counting the number of faces, edges and vertices (corners). Prisms and pyramids can cause confusion. A pyramid has triangular sides that meet at a point. The base shape gives its name e.g. 'square-based pyramid'. A prism has two end shapes that are identical and rectangular sides. A triangular prism has two triangle end faces and three rectangular side faces.

Unit 28: Nets of 3D solids   The net of a 3D solid is what it looks like when it is opened out flat. Encourage your child to picture opening out a box. If it were closed up, it could be opened again so that the net would look different. Point out that solids can have more than one net. In order to recognise solids from their nets, your child will need to know the shapes of the faces and the number of faces of different 3D solids.

Unit 29: Angles and lines   There are three key rules for angles that your child needs to know. Make sure that he or she knows what an angle is and is able to recognise different sizes of angles. For example, can your child recognise 180°, 90°, 60°, 45°? Once your child is a good angle estimator, he or she needs to be able to use a protractor and then learn these angle properties. Angles in a straight line adding to 180° is an important rule and this can help your child to learn the other two rules. To check if the angles of a triangle add up to 180°, cut out a triangle and then cut off each corner. Arrange the corners by placing them next to each other to make a straight line.

Unit 30: Symmetry   A mirror line or line of symmetry is best thought of as a line that cuts a shape into two identical pieces. If a mirror is placed on the line, the whole shape would be seen when you looked in the mirror. Some shapes have only one line of symmetry, but other shapes have more, such as equilateral triangles and regular hexagons, or no lines of symmetry.

Unit 31: Coordinates   A common error when reading coordinates is to get the two numbers the wrong way around. In the example, position (3, 5) is shown as B. Encourage your child to start at the zero and go across the horizontal x-axis until level with the B (across 3) and then up to B (up 5). This will get your child into the habit of reading across the x-axis before going up the y-axis. It is the same for negative numbers – read across and then up.

Unit 32: Reflection   A reflection is the image seen in a mirror. A shape with two halves that are mirror images has reflection or line symmetry. The coordinate grid needs to be used to work out the exact position of each reflected point. The best strategy is to count the number of squares from each point in the mirror line and then count the same number of squares on the other side of the line. The result can be checked with a mirror.

Unit 33: Measures   The metric system is a system of weights and measures. All the units in the metric system are in tens, hundreds and thousands, which makes it a lot easier to convert between measures than with the old imperial system. Millimetres, metres, millilitres, litres, grams and kilograms are all examples of units in the metric system. Check that your child is able to convert fractions of quantities, such as halves, quarters and tenths of centimetres, metres, litres or kilograms.

Unit 34: Area and perimeter   Your child should be able to use the two formulae for working out the area and perimeter of a rectangle. Make sure that your child understands that we use just the initial letters to represent the words – for example, l is length and w is width. Check that area and perimeter aren't confused, and remind your child that area is measured in square centimetres (cm^2) or square metres (m^2).

Unit 35: Area – compound shapes   Your child should be able to use the formula for working out the area of a rectangle. Make sure that your child understands that we use just the initial letters to represent the words – for example, l is length and w is width. A compound shape made from several rectangles (for example, the plan of a house) can be split into rectangles so that the areas of each of these can be totalled.

Unit 36: Volume   Your child should be able to use the formula for working out the volume of a cuboid. It is useful to think of the volume as the area of the base multiplied by the height, as this formula will work for any prism or cylinder. The area of the base of a cuboid is length $\times$ width, so another way of thinking about the volume is length $\times$ width $\times$ height (l $\times$ w $\times$ h). Make sure that your child knows that volume is measured in cubic centimetres (cm^3) or cubic metres (m^3).

Unit 37: Time   Your child needs to be able to relate the 24-hour clock to the 12-hour clock with a.m. and p.m. Remind your child that 24-hour time always has four digits. From midnight until midday (a.m. times) the two systems use the same numbers e.g. 7.45 a.m. = 07:45 and 10.25 a.m. = 10:25. From midday the 24-hour clock continues on to 13:00, 14:00, etc. up to midnight. The time is, in effect, written with an extra 12 hours added e.g. 2.15 p.m. = 14:15 and 9.35 p.m. = 21:35.

Unit 38: Timetables   Your child needs to be able to read the 24-hour clock, particularly on timetables, and relate it to the 12-hour clock. Remind your child that 24-hour time always has four digits. When you are given a start time and finish time and need to calculate the length of a journey, it helps to picture a time line in your head. For example, a journey starts at 15:40 and finishes at 17:05 – 15:40 ➡ (add 20 mins) ➡ 16:00 ➡ (add 1 hr 5 mins) ➡ 17:05. The journey lasts 1 hour 25 minutes.

Unit 39: Data – line graphs   Line graphs have points plotted which are then joined with a line. Encourage your child to read them by going up from the horizontal axis to meet the line and then from this point across to the vertical axis to give the value. Make sure that your child understands that the scale on graphs can alter. It is important to read all the information about each graph, such as the title and axis headings, in order to have a good understanding of the graph.

Unit 40: Data – averages   There are three types of average – mode (most common), median (middle) and mean (total divided by number of items). Sometimes these three are the same number, but sometimes they are different. Check that your child understands the difference between them. Mode and median are relatively easy to work out, particularly if the list of numbers is put in order first. The mean is the one that involves calculating, by finding the total and dividing by the number of items.

Answers

Unit 1: Decimal numbers (page 6)

1 a $\frac{6}{10}$ b $\frac{5}{100}$

   c $\frac{3}{10}$ d $\frac{2}{1000}$

   e $\frac{5}{1000}$ f $\frac{7}{10}$

   g $\frac{4}{1000}$ h $\frac{2}{100}$

2 a 0.03   0.05   0.1   0.14   0.19
   b 3.01   3.04   3.07   3.12   3.18

3 1.068

Unit 2: Decimals – place value (page 7)

1 a 42   195   7.5   18.73 3.66
   b 435   960   251   7.2   340.6
   c 1.84   1.38   0.96   0.025 0.703
   d 0.191 0.8   0.715 0.082 0.007

2 a 0.45   0.045   4.5
   b 20.6   0.206   2.06
   c 0.033   3.3   0.33
   d 162   16.2   0.162

Unit 3: Ordering numbers (page 8)

1 a 2.05   5.03   5.23   5.35   5.7
   b 1.27   1.3   2.68   2.81   3.88
   c 4.77   40.77 47.07 47.4   47.7
   d 2.06   2.3   2.83   23.11 23.3
   e 6.12   6.21   6.5   6.65   7.03
   f 19.29 19.5   20.05 20.53 20.9
   g 3.09   3.23   3.68   3.81   3.9
   h 13.09 13.95 14.09 14.37 14.4

2 Check that your child's eight
   numbers are in order, starting with
   the smallest. Also check that he or
   she has used only the digits 3, 6, 9,
   2 and a decimal point, and that all
   the numbers are between 1 and 10.

Unit 4: Number sequences (page 9)

b −4   7   40   Rule: +11
c   2   −6   −18   Rule: −4
d −35   −15   45   Rule: +20
e   7   −14   −21   Rule: −7
f 16   −8   −20   Rule: −12
g −52   −22   68   Rule: +30
h   7   −2   −29   Rule: −9

Unit 5: Function machines (page 10)

1 a   0   3   6   9   12   15   18
   b −1   1   3   5   7   9   11
   c −4 −3 −2 −1   0   1   2
   d   1   4   7   10   13   16   19
   e   4   6   8   10   12   14   16
   f −3   2   7   12   17   22   27

2 a −3   b × 2 + 5
   c × 3 − 1   d × 3 + 6 or + 2 × 3

Unit 6: Multiples (page 11)

1 a 136   b 4314   c 4124   d 3509

2 a

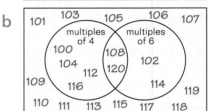

   b

3 360 can be exactly divided by: 2, 3,
   4, 5, 6, 8, 9, and 10.

Unit 7: Factors (page 12)

1 a (1,15) (3,5)
   b (1,8)   (2,4)
   c (1,28) (2,14) (4,7)
   d (1,45) (3,15) (5,9)
   e (1,20) (2,10) (4,5)
   f (1,32) (2,16) (4, 8)
   g (1,30) (2,15) (3,10) (5,6)
   h (1,42) (2,21) (3,14) (6,7)
   i (1,40) (2,20) (4,10) (5,8)
   j (1,48) (2,24) (3,16) (4,12) (6,8)

2 a 1,5,25   b 1,2,3,4,6,9,12,18,36
   c 1,7,49   d 1,2,4,8,16,32,64
   e The number of factors of
   squared numbers is always odd
   e.g. 16 has 5 factors.

3 a 17 and 19   b 20
   c 16   d 18 and 21
   e 18   f 21

58

Unit 8: Fractions (page 13)

1 a 6   b 5   c 3   d 12
   e 5   f 1   g 4   h 18

2 There are many answers but these are some possible answers.

a $\frac{2}{6}$ $\frac{3}{9}$ $\frac{4}{12}$ b $\frac{2}{8}$ $\frac{3}{12}$ $\frac{4}{16}$

c $\frac{6}{8}$ $\frac{9}{12}$ $\frac{12}{16}$ d $\frac{4}{6}$ $\frac{6}{9}$ $\frac{8}{12}$

3 a $\frac{15}{20}$ b $\frac{12}{20}$ c $\frac{9}{24}$

Unit 9: Ordering fractions (page 14)

1 a $\frac{5}{8}$ b $\frac{3}{10}$ c $\frac{5}{6}$

d $\frac{7}{8}$ e $\frac{5}{6}$ f $\frac{1}{2}$

g $\frac{1}{4}$ h $\frac{2}{3}$ i $\frac{3}{4}$

j $\frac{5}{6}$

2 a $\frac{1}{3}$ $\frac{5}{12}$ $\frac{1}{2}$ $\frac{3}{4}$ $\frac{5}{6}$

b $\frac{1}{15}$ $\frac{1}{3}$ $\frac{7}{15}$ $\frac{2}{3}$ $\frac{4}{5}$

c $\frac{1}{6}$ $\frac{1}{2}$ $\frac{7}{12}$ $\frac{2}{3}$ $\frac{3}{4}$

d $\frac{1}{6}$ $\frac{2}{9}$ $\frac{1}{2}$ $\frac{5}{9}$ $\frac{2}{3}$

e $\frac{1}{2}$ $\frac{3}{5}$ $\frac{7}{10}$ $\frac{3}{4}$ $\frac{4}{5}$

f $\frac{3}{8}$ $\frac{5}{8}$ $\frac{2}{3}$ $\frac{3}{4}$ $\frac{5}{6}$

Unit 10: Fractions and decimals (page 15)

1 a 0.4   b 0.7   c 0.125
   d 0.8   e 0.625

2 a $\frac{9}{10}$ b $\frac{3}{10}$ c $\frac{17}{20}$

d $\frac{3}{20}$ e $\frac{1}{100}$

3 $3.2 \rightarrow 3\frac{1}{5}$ $2.8 \rightarrow 2\frac{4}{5}$

$3.5 \rightarrow 3\frac{1}{2}$ $2.7 \rightarrow 2\frac{7}{10}$

$3.4 \rightarrow 3\frac{2}{5}$ $2.75 \rightarrow 2\frac{3}{4}$

$3.25 \rightarrow 3\frac{1}{4}$ $2.125 \rightarrow 2\frac{1}{8}$

Unit 11: Percentages (page 16)

1 a 70%   b 75%   c 80%
   d 68%   e 95%   f 60%
   g 15%   h 92%

2 a 3   b 1   c 3
   d 9   e 9   f 1
   g 3   h 49

3 a 1%   b 80%   c 80%
   d 70%   e 72%   f 80%

Unit 12: Percentages of amounts (page 17)

1 a 14p   28p   7p
   b 38p   76p   19p
   c 52p   £1.04   26p
   d £1.26   £2.52   63p
   e £2.80   £5.60   £1.40
   f £2.36   £4.72   £1.18
   g £1.90   £3.80   95p
   h £2.12   £4.24   £1.06

2 a 60 cm   b 75 litres   c 15   d 16

Unit 13: Number facts (page 18)

1
	a	b	c	d
	8	7	7	8
	18	27	37	28
	80	70	70	80

   e 9   f 9   g 11   h 12
    9   9   21   42
    90   90   110   120

2
a	b	c	d	e
15	6	17	12	8
13	9	12	6	6
4	11	16	5	16
7	13	18	14	7

Unit 14: Brackets (page 19)

1 a 49   b 4   c 24
   d 21   e 3   f 35
   g 5   h 7   i 12

2
  a $(7 + 3) \times 8 = 80$
  b $(6 - 2) \times (8 + 3) = 44$
  c $8 + (4 - 2) \times 3 = 30$
  d $8 + (10 \div 2) \times 3 = 39$
  e $(40 \div 5) \times 4 = 32$

3
  a $5 \times (3 + 9) = 60$
  b $3 + (19 - 8) = 14$
  c $(6 \times 4) - (16 \div 4) = 20$
  d $(4 \times 5) + (3 \times 8) = 44$
  e $(9 + 8) - (2 \times 6) = 5$
  f $8 + (7 \times 3) - 9 = 20$

Unit 15: Addition (page 20)

1

a	7404	b	7700
c	3968	d	8709
e	8691	f	8216
g	12 234	h	8146
i	13 382	j	13 240

2

a
```
    4 3 7 2
  + 1 6 8 5
    6 0 5 7
```
b
```
    4 8 0 5
  + 3 9 9 7
    8 8 0 2
```

c
```
    7 3 9 4
  + 1 8 7 3
    9 2 6 7
```
d
```
    5 3 4 5
  + 7 4 1 5
  1 2 7 6 0
```

e
```
    5 2 7 7
  + 8 3 4 4
  1 3 6 2 1
```
f
```
    6 3 2 7
  + 5 9 7 5
  1 2 3 0 2
```

3
  a $3224 + 6934 + 9842$
  b $4601 + 7020 + 8379$

Unit 16: Subtraction (page 21)

1

a	1849	b	1454	c	3408
d	4891	e	2825	f	6630
g	3644	h	11 210	i	35 544
j	17 450				

2

a
```
    7 3 7 5
  − 2 9 8 7
    4 3 8 8
```
b
```
    5 0 6 4
  − 2 8 6 5
    2 1 9 9
```

c
```
    6 2 0 1
  − 3 6 4 6
    2 5 5 5
```
d
```
  1 0 4 7 3
  −   8 5 6 5
    1 9 0 8
```

e
```
  3 4 3 6 1
  −   7 6 7 7
  2 6 6 8 4
```
f
```
  4 5 0 0 4
  − 1 4 6 8 5
  3 0 3 1 9
```

3
  $4735 \rightarrow 10\,290$
  $11\,200 \rightarrow 5645$
  $6830 \rightarrow 12\,385$
  $3845 \rightarrow 9400$

Unit 17: Addition and subtraction (page 22)

a Fred's score

Total	Score
82	343
108	235
95	140
105	35
34	1

b Joe's score

Total	Score
61	345
106	239
56	183
51	132
132	0

The winner is Joe.

Unit 18: Decimal addition and subtraction (page 23)

1
  a

Event	Total
Vault	74.91
Balance	75.96
Bars	70.62
Floor	77.39

  b

Gymnast	Total
Yalena	75.04
Beatrice	74.58
Nadia	74.02
Becky	75.24

2 Gold – Becky
Silver – Yalena
Bronze – Beatrice

3
  a 0.66
  b 6.77
  c Becky and Yalena
  d 2.59

Unit 19: Money calculations (page 24)

1 a £22.99   b £19.49
   c £22.79   d £5.85
   e £14.79   f £3.19

2 They need to visit 8 times.

Unit 20: Mental multiplication (page 25)

1 a 120   b 400   c 180   d 180
    152   456   192   186
   e 420
    444

2 a 237   b 504   c 380
   d 376   e 567

3 a 34.2 cm²   b 23.5 cm²
   c 20.4 cm²   d 73.6 cm²

Unit 21: Written multiplication (page 26)

1 a 3604   b 4558   c 4608
   d 2242   e 3772   f 2886

2 a £8.50   b £12.06   c £13.05
   d £23.36

Unit 22: Division with remainders (page 27)

1 a 81 r 2   b 77 r 1   c 47 r 1
   d 87   e 73 r 2   f 51 r 4
   g 34 r 2   h 132 r 1   i 162 r 2

2 a 116 and 780   b 780 and 425
   c 780 and 762   d 677 and 425
   e 677 and 762   f 116, 677 and
                               425

3 a $\begin{array}{r} 7\ 2 \\ 3\overline{)2\ 1\ 6} \end{array}$ b $\begin{array}{r} 8\ 3 \\ 4\overline{)3\ 3\ 2} \end{array}$

Unit 23: Division – decimal answers (page 28)

1 a 38.6   b 34.5   c 108.75
   d 61.4   e 82.2   f 159.5
   g 35.625   h 159.75

2 a 43.33   b 49.17   c 25.43
   d 85.44   e 47.17   f 204.67
   g 42.11   h 58.29

3 a $\begin{array}{r} 73.25 \\ 8\overline{)586} \end{array}$ b $\begin{array}{r} 54.75 \\ 4\overline{)219} \end{array}$

Unit 24: Money problems (page 29)

1 a £14.34   b £140.55
   c £18.35   d £24.72

2 a £2.76   b £9.24
   c £2.39   d £8.96

Unit 25: 2D shapes – quadrilaterals (page 30)

1 a square   b rectangle

   c rhombus   d parallelogram

   e trapzium   f kite

   g parallelogram   h trapezium

2 Check that each shape is a quadrilateral.

Unit 26: 2D shapes – polygons (page 31)

shape	sketch	number of sides	number of right angles	number of lines of symmetry
rectangle		4	4	2
equilateral triangle		3	0	3
rhombus		4	0	2
isosceles triangle		3	0	1
regular hexagon		6	0	6
square		4	4	4
kite		4	2, 1 or 0	1
parallelogram		4	0	0

Unit 27: 3D solids (page 32)

1

Shape	a	b	c	d	e	f	g	h
Prism	✓			✓		✓		✓
Pyramid		✓	✓		✓		✓	

2
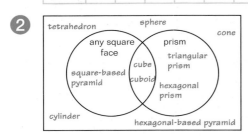

Unit 28: Nets of 3D solids (page 33)

1
  a cuboid
  b tetrahedron or triangular-based pyramid
  c square-based pyramid
  d triangular prism
  e cube
  f pentagonal-based pyramid

2 Check that your child's nets have six equal square sides and can be folded to make a cube.

Unit 29: Angles and lines (page 34)

1
a 65°	b 25°	c 40°
d 68°	e 56°	f 25°
g 21°	h 104°	

2
a 142°	b 28°	c 90°
d 98°, 82°	e 154°, 26°	f 108°

Unit 30: Symmetry (page 35)

1
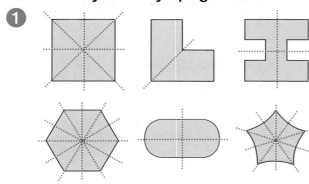

2 Check that your child's colouring is symmetrical. Use a mirror to help.

Unit 31: Coordinates (page 36)

1
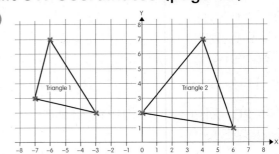

2 a A → (−2, 8)   B → (6, 4)
     b Check that the points have been plotted correctly. The shape is a parallelogram.

Unit 32: Reflection (page 37)

1 Check that the triangle drawn has these coordinates: (7, 3) (11, 1) (10, 8).

2 Check that the first quadrilateral has been plotted correctly. The reflected quadrilateral coordinates are: (5, 1) (8, 0) (5, 3) (2, 0).

3 The reflected pentagon coordinates are: (7, 0) (4, 0) (1, 2) (4, 4) (7, 4).

Unit 33: Measures (page 38)

1
a 350 cm	b 1900 g	c 142 mm
d 250 ml	e 2750 m	f 600 g
g 4750 ml	h 7300 m	

2
a <	b >	c =	d <
e >	f >	g >	h =

Unit 34: Area and perimeter (page 39)

1
a 28 cm²	22 cm
b 54 cm²	30 cm
c 20 cm²	18 cm
d 24 cm²	22 cm

2 a perimeter = 24 cm
        area = 36 cm²
     b 36 cm
     c 144 cm²

Unit 35: Area – compound shapes (page 40)

a 192 cm²   b 143 cm²   c 165 cm²
d 95 cm²   e 176 cm²   f 137 cm²
g 71 cm²   h 124 cm²

Unit 36: Volume (page 41)

1 a 480 cm³   b 72 cm³   c 90 cm³
       d 60 cm³   e 32 cm³   f 250 cm³
       g 48 cm³   h 490 cm³

2

length	width	height	volume
8 cm	4 cm	3 cm	**96 cm³**
5 cm	2 cm	**6 cm**	60 cm³
10 cm	9 cm	4 cm	360 cm³
8 cm	**3 cm**	2 cm	48 cm³
4 cm	3 cm	7 cm	**84 cm³**
10 cm	6 cm	**3 cm**	180 cm³

Unit 37: Time (page 42)

1 a 07:20   b 16:15   c 21:05
       d 11:30   e 13:40   f 14:53
       g 06:03   h 15:48   i 10:41

2 a 2.55 p.m.   b 5.20 p.m.   c 2.05 a.m.
       d 11.40 a.m.   e 1.25 p.m.   f 6.14 a.m.
       g 9.53 p.m.   h 10.28 a.m.   i 3.04 p.m.

3

Unit 38: Timetables (page 43)

a 17:26
b Train 2, the 15:30 from King's Cross
c 4
d 2 hours 21 minutes
e 17:14
f Darlington
g 2 hours 17 minutes
h 1 hour 39 minutes

Unit 39: Data – line graphs (page 44)

1 Answers are approximate.

°F	50	178	150	77	65	86	90	108
°C	10	80	65	25	18	30	32	42

2 a 19 °C   b September
       c 18 °C   d December
       e June

Unit 40: Data – averages (page 45)

1 a £19 £26 £28 £32 £32 £32 £41
       b £32   c £32   d £30

2 a 78° 79° 80° 80° 81° 81° 81°
       b 81°   c 80°   d 80°

Test 1 (pages 46 and 47)

1 a 1.06   b 1.17

2 1   −7   −31

3 a 14.5 cm   b 2.65 kg
       c 5.25 m or $5\frac{1}{4}$ m
       d 6.2 litres

4 a £2.40   b €10

5 a 8   b 62   c 60

6 $\frac{2}{3} = \frac{20}{30} = \frac{6}{9} = \frac{14}{21} = \frac{30}{45}$

7

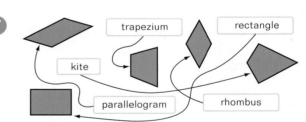

8

12-hour	24-hour
7.25 a.m.	**07.25**
7.50 p.m.	19:50
3.32 p.m.	**15.32**
10.39 a.m.	10:39

9 14 057

10 4850

Test 2 (pages 48 and 49)

1 25.9   29.05   29.29   29.35   29.5

2 × 3 − 5   10   13

③ 240 cm³

④ a 39p   b 39p   c 40p

⑤ a 1   b 10

⑥ $\frac{1}{2}$ $\frac{2}{3}$ $\frac{7}{10}$ $\frac{4}{5}$ $\frac{5}{6}$

⑦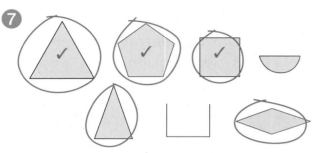

⑧ a 19 minutes   b 47 minutes

⑨ a 36.02   b 262.58

⑩ a 17.58   b 23.72

Test 3 (pages 50 and 51)

① 144   276   216

② perimeter = 40 cm
area = 91 cm²

③ a 304   b 43.2

④ a 72 r 4 or 72.8
b 138 r 3 or 138.5

⑤ a Odd one out = square-based pyramid, the rest are prisms
b Odd one out = triangular prism, the rest are pyramids

⑥ A → (−5, 3)   B → (0, 5)

⑦ a 0.6   b $\frac{1}{4}$
c 0.7   d $\frac{1}{50}$ (or $\frac{2}{100}$)

⑧ a 60%   b 35%   c 78%

⑨
```
mirror graph
```

⑩ £7.27

Test 4 (pages 52 and 53)

① a (1,45) (3,15) (5,9)
b (1,30) (2,15) (3,10) (5,6)

② 61 cm²

③ a 1802   b 3042

④ a 76.4   b 61.875

⑤ a cuboid   b square-based pyramid

⑥ A (−4, −2)   B (−3, 1)

⑦ a 138.5   b 76.2   c 1.49   d 0.7

⑧ a 36p 72p 18p
b 24p 72p 36p

⑨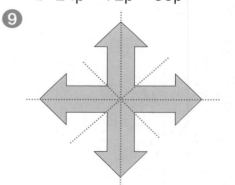

⑩ a £1.25   b £29.58

64